©2016 by Wendel T. Dandridge
All rights reserved. No part of this book may be produced or transmitted in any form or by any means, electronic or mechanical, including photocopying, recording, or by any information storage or retrieval system, without written permission from People Publishing except for the inclusion of quotations in a review.

Library of Congress Cataloging-In-Publication Data

Returning to the Message of Christ:

Re-Establishing Church and Christian Relevancy through Christ Consciousness, Social Justice and Humanitarian Responsibility

Table of Contents

i. The Death and Decline of Christianity and the Church (7)
    a. How have Christians become dead to humanity? (15)
    b. The absence of Christians in the community (19)
    c. How modern day Christians compare to the original believers (26)
    d. Why aren't Christians involved in the church or community? (32)

ii. What are the issues facing humanity today? (35)
    a. Homelessness (39)
    b. Human sex trafficking and exploitation (49)
    c. Lack of clean water in developing countries. (54)
    d. Domestic violence (62)
    e. HIV/AIDS (68)
    f. Global illiteracy (73)

iii. Explaining the decline in church attendance (79)
    a. How Super Christians can become Dead Christians. (85)
    b. The message to become a "follower" of Christ (91)
    c. The entertainment of ministry as a smoke screen to true service. (105)
    d. How modern millennials and intellectuals view church (110)

iv. What is God telling believers and non-believers? (127)
    a. Christians as active human agents in humanity. (137)
    b. The cost of service for the Christian believer (148)
    c. Re-establishing a sense of community: "The US Factor" (159)
    d. The brand of Christianity in the eyes of humanity. (166)

v. Developing Christ consciousness (173)
    a. Good won't get it (181)
    b. Jesus' call to action (185)
    c. Jesus as a champion for social justice. (189)
    d. Jesus' push for equality (194)
    e. How Jesus brought light to the real issues of humanity and community. (196)
    f. Jesus' push for human rights over political rights. (198)
    g. Jesus: A man for the oppressed (201)
    h. Jesus: A man for the disinherited (204)
    i. Jesus: A man for the disenfranchised (207)
    j. Jesus as advocate for the greatest sense of community (209)
    k. A proclamation of good news to the poor (211)
    l. Liberty and healing for humanity begins "in the year of our lord" (215)

vi. Methods and practices of outreach and relevancy (225)

THE DEATH & DECLINE OF CHRISTIANITY AND THE CHURCH

If you aren't in the medical field you probably are unaware that there is certain protocol in order to pronounce someone dead. Believe it or not there are actual templates that doctors and physicians will use in order to ensure that a death pronouncement has been done properly. In my personal research I was able to discover that there are 5 specific things that need to take place for an effective declaration of death:

1. Correctly identify the patient.
2. Note that the patient is NOT hypothermic. The individual has to be warm and dead.
3. Note that there is no spontaneous movement. No verbal or tactile stimulation. No pupillary light reflex. No breathing or lung sounds. And that there is no heartbeat or pulse.
4. Communicate with the family, notify the organ donor, post mortem services, autopsy or chaplain.
5. Notify the coroner. This should be done within 24 hours with the cause of death being expresses at natural, unusual circumstances or trauma.

It is interesting to note that many of the above mentioned things we can actually parallel to the present day church. As a matter of fact I would like to, as a licensed and ordained Pastor in the Christian church, make an official proclamation of the Dead Christian. I am sure I can use the same template used by physicians:

"I have been called to the bedside of the church to pronounce that patient Christian has died. No spontaneous movements were present. There was no response to verbal or tactile stimuli. Pupils were mid-dilated and fixed. No breath sounds were appreciated over either lung field. No carotid pulses were palpable. No heart sounds were auscultator over entire precordium. Patient pronounced dead at present day. Family and resident were notified. Chaplain and post mortem services offered. The family has declined organ donation. Patient's major medical illness was **relevancy.** Confirmed and witnessed by God's eyes"

You are right to assume that this text will be a little hard hitting on the plight that I believe is facing the existence of Christianity. Every year there are countless people who, not only stray away from organized religion but also, lose their faith. I believe this decline in faith is not just related to faith in God but also faith in humanity. As we continue to view and face terroristic acts, poverty, genocide and health disparities, people are asking the serious questions about human agency in the world. They are asking, "Where is God?"

I am sure there are some people who will critique these words as slightly harsh towards the church. However, I believe that these words are precisely what the church universal needs to hear. Engage with me in a small synopsis and critique of the vocabulary I chose to use in the declaration of death to "Christian".

1. "The bedside of the church". I believe the church has been on its sickbed for some time. It has become evident that many churches have become revolving doors for people searching for hope and action in humanity. Christianity has become a religion that has struggled to remain relevant to this millennial generation.
2. "No spontaneous movements". What major advancements have been made by Christians in the last 50 years that would warrant the title of a movement? What major historical events can be pinpointed to Christian influence? A spontaneous movement is one unexpected. What have Christians done do shake up the culture of current society?

3. "No response to verbal or tactile stimuli". How long has the church, and Christians, heard the cries of community to serve, but have turned a deaf ear to the true needs of humanity? There are countless causes that have called for the presence of Christians. Unfortunately their return message has been silence.

4. "Pupils were mid-dilated and fixed". It is interesting to note where the focus of many Christians and churches have gone; to self. The Christian community has become focused on self-preservation instead of preservation of The Great Commission established by Jesus.

5. "No breath sounds". Many churches and Christians have become silent to the issues that perplex the world and the communities they are located in. "No breath sounds" translates to silence. The religious community has become mute regarding issues that affect humanity.

6. "No carotid pulses". Where is the pulse of Christianity? Where is the pulse of the church? How, and why, it is that Christian service is no longer felt in our communities? A pulse is determined by what the practitioner feels on the outside of the body in order to determine the internal functions. The "feel" of Christianity can be felt from the inside of the church walls. What I seek to uncover is how the pulse is felt by those who are on the outside of the church.

7. "No heart sounds were auscultator". Where is the heartbeat of God being heard in the actions of the church and Christians? In order to confirm the pulse of the body the sound of the heart must be heard. It is possible that what is felt via the pulse isn't consistent with what is actually occurring in the body. This has become true with the church universal.

8. "Patient's major medical illness was relevancy". There was a time when Christians had an impact in the world and in humanity at large. What significant relationships are still present today? The illness of the church and Christianity is significance. If we are going to revive the faith in humanity we will have to revisit the importance of Christianity in humanity.

I am beginning to notice a trend amongst people who profess to be Christians. They do nothing, or very little, that would be evidence to their profession of faith. I'm not talking about church attendance, prayer time, scripture reading, and worship participation. These are all things most Christians are good at. These faith displays are simple to execute for most people. While reluctant some weeks, it's fairly easy to find a church service to attend. Talking to God can be done at any point in the day. The bible is the best-selling book in history. However, I would like to address the heart of Christianity that I personally see taking its last breath; service to humanity.

As we look out into the world are we seeing the love of God displayed? As the need for moral consciousness rises, who is taking the lead in serving the disparities of the world? There are countless Christians, and devote religious people, who profess faith. However I am concerned with the number of those who actually act out their profession. Service to humanity, in my opinion, is the heart of Christianity. To me it is the root and pure essence of our existence. In the pages to follow we are going to discover how service is not just our Christian responsibility but also our human obligation.

That's right! I don't think the problem is church attendance or church participation for Christians. I do believe personal devotion is important in the life of a Christian. However, the heartbeat of God is slowly leaving the earth because I believe the hands and feet of God (Christians) have become lazy in the areas of community service and missions projects. Dead Christians have become silent to the social and economic injustices that still plague the globe. Media doesn't mention many of these disparities anymore, and social media has become so flooded with narcissistic posts that we have lost the consciousness that service to humanity is still necessary.

Ezekiel is placed in a very similar observation when he visits the Valley of Dry Bones:

> [1]The lord took hold of me, and I was carried away by the Spirit of the lord to a valley filled with bones. [2]He led me all around among the bones that covered the valley floor. They were scattered everywhere across the ground and were completely dried out. [3]Then

he asked me, "Son of man, can these bones become living people again?"

"O Sovereign lord," I replied, "you alone know the answer to that." ⁴Then he said to me, "Speak a prophetic message to these bones and say, 'Dry bones, listen to the word of the lord! ⁵This is what the Sovereign lord says: Look! I am going to put breath into you and make you live again! ⁶I will put flesh and muscles on you and cover you with skin. I will put breath into you, and you will come to life. Then you will know that I am the lord.'"

⁷So I spoke this message, just as he told me. Suddenly as I spoke, there was a rattling noise all across the valley. The bones of each body came together and attached themselves as complete skeletons. ⁸Then as I watched, muscles and flesh formed over the bones. Then skin formed to cover their bodies, but they still had no breath in them.

⁹Then he said to me, "Speak a prophetic message to the winds, son of man. Speak a prophetic message and say, 'This is what the Sovereign lord says: Come, O breath, from the four winds! Breathe into these dead bodies so they may live again.'"

¹⁰So I spoke the message as he commanded me, and breath came into their bodies. They all came to life and stood up on their feet—a great army.

¹¹Then he said to me, "Son of man, these bones represent the people of Israel. They are saying, 'We have become old, dry bones—all hope is gone. Our nation is finished.' ¹²Therefore, prophesy to them and say, 'This is what the Sovereign lord says: O my people, I will open your graves of exile and cause you to rise again. Then I will bring you back to the land of Israel. ¹³When this happens, O my people, you will know that I am the lord. ¹⁴I will put my Spirit in you, and you will live again and return home to your own land. Then you will know that I, the lord, have spoken, and I have done what I said. Yes, the lord has spoken!'" Ezekiel 37:1-14 (New Living Translation)

There are a few elements of this text that I believe deserve our attention. The first observation is that God takes the prophet and places him in the place where he is to receive his revelation. This could suggest to us that God will take us to the place in which He wants to use us. In the event that we are unwilling to go on our own, there are forces greater than us that will lead us to the places and communities where we need to be. Whether it through circumstance of religious quest I believe that God will do what God needs to do in order to make us aware of the dead situations that are happening around us. The bible says that he takes the prophet and places him right in the center of the valley. There are social, economic, environmental and ethical issues that I believe God wants to place us in the middle of in order to bring these disparities to the fore front of our minds. There are Christians, and various churches, that find themselves in the heart of these contemporary valleys of dry bones. Unfortunately, they have not made the conscious decision to speak life.

The second point is that the bones were located in a valley. We have come to know a valley for being a place that is located between two mountainous ranges. I find it interesting that dry bones would be located in a place that is typically rich in moisture. Ecology has proven that valleys thrive off of the water flow that comes down from the mountains. Most valleys are known to have a stream running through them. So how could these dry bones be dry if they are in a place of moisture? Or could this text be painting a larger picture for our consideration. Could this illustration point us to the truth that in present day, with all the rich and fruitful resources we have at our disposal, there are some communities and people who have become parched and dehydrated because of our unwillingness to share the living waters of Christ?

A personification of God is further shown when God takes the prophet and gives him a tour of the dry bones. God walks with the prophet in order to show him what the issues are in the valley. God takes the prophet by the hand and gives him a fair assessment of what he has been dropped into. Isn't it just like God to drop you into an environment and then show you specifically what the issues are? I believe, as it relates to the modern day quandaries that will be discussed in this text, that God has made it very clear of our assignment. I believe that God wants us to have a great understanding of what the great commission is to look like in the world. When we are doing the work the work of Christ there should be no ambiguity as to what the core of our assignment is.

What happens next in the text, I believe, is the greatest part of the story for us in the modern world. God challenged the prophet with the question, "Can these bones live again?". God's inquiry is a reminder that God will openly give us a test in order to gauge our capacity for enlightenment. Simply put, God wants to see what our perception is about the reality He has placed us in. Even God understands that it is not our reality that we must live with; however, it is our perception of our realities that become the driving force for our actions. God asks the prophet this question in order to test his faith. God is using the same method with present Christians and the church. We will discuss later in this text how Jesus simplifies the challenge of God into one great commandment. God needs to know who is willing to act when it is apparent that the situations are dead.

Once God tests the willingness and faith of the prophet, God then challenges the obedience of Ezekiel. God instructs the prophet to speak a prophetic message to a valley of dry bones. What we must note in this instruction is that there will be times in our lives where God will instruct us to speak to environments that appear dead. This is the purpose of this text. At first perception, we may feel as though God is sending us unto environment and places that are well past their life expectancy. I believe the relevancy of Christianity and the church is centered on our ability to speak to lifeless situations and to bring hope. Unfortunately, many Christians and churches have been unwilling to be obedient to the voice and challenge of God to speak to the dry bones of today. The message in the days of the prophet Ezekiel should be the same words on the tongues Christians today. We have been commissioned to speak the word that God wants to put breath back into lifeless situations, communities and environments.

We note in this text that there was a rattling noise which signified that God was working. If true Christians were alive today there would be a sound of God to indicate that His presence was active on the earth. I will discuss this later in the text, however the presence of God through Christians is no longer felt or heard in our current society. And if it is present the voice is that of an ant instead of a roaring lion. What happens next in the text is perplexing but offers us a modern day revelation.

The bible says that the bones joined together and skin was formed but there was no life. As it relates to the context of this text, there are many people who profess to be a part of the body of Christ but have no life. We have declared dead what thinks itself to be alive. It wasn't until the prophet spoke that breath entered the bodies. It will not be until other voices like mine speak to where we can see a difference and a change in humanity. Finally, what was a valley of dry bones soon became an army. Imagine the impact that will be made on the world and humanity the moment "Dead Christians" become alive, acting, living, and breathing organisms for change.

HOW HAVE CHRISTIANS BECOME DEAD TO HUMANITY?

Studies have actually shown over the years a decline in Christianity as a religion. I believe the lack of service is the main cause for its degeneration. In my humble opinion **Christians have become dead to humanity.** Napp Nazworth, Christian Post Reporter, writes, "The decline in Americans who identify as Christian shown by a new Pew report is mostly due to those with weak church ties no longer identifying as Christian."[1] There was a time in culture where a person could easily identify a Christian. To the same degree, as I will later speak on, there was a time when those professing Christianity could be easily identified. You would make the assumption based on what you saw being done in the environment you were observing. Interesting enough, this supposition wasn't made by a person's church attendance or by their personal devotion. However, in history past there was a time Christians were known by their works.

When we look at and analyze the early church, the Christian community was known for what they did and not for their worship. Keep in mind the formation of the church we are familiar with today did not take full formation until many years pasted from Jesus' death and resurrection. Later in this text we will analyze the early church as it compares to modern day ministries. The congregations we have come to know today took time to develop. The liturgies and worship experiences we have today were not present in the early church. There was no praise and worship team or choir. There was no hype man or worship presider. There was no order of worship. There were Pastors and Deacons and Elders, however their job descriptions involved service to the community and were not likened to the job descriptions of a corporate CEO. There were no budget meetings taking place.

---

[1] Nazworth, Napp. 2015. *CP U.S.* May 15. www.christianpost.com/news/is-christian-decline-in-america-due-to-fewer-incognito-atheists-like-russsell-moore-said-cp-asked-pew-research-for-the-answer-139133/.

The above mentioned elements of church today took time to formulate. Yes, the message of Jesus' resurrection, and the house meetings, were a part of the Christian movement. However the birth of the church took place in the book of "Acts" for a reason. People knew that God was real, and the spirit of God was present on the earth, through the **works** of Christians. People weren't running to Christianity in order to get a spiritual high or to have a worship experience. People were attracted to this movement because it was centered on the altruistic acts of service and selflessness.

There was a point in history where if you heard of a house being built for a single mother in a low income neighborhood you would assume Christians were building it. If you saw people in the city doing a clothing drive or feeding the homeless you would assume they were Christians. If you heard of a father being reunited with his family after completing a drug program, you would assume the program was provided by the church. If there was an issue of crime in an area where a church was present, there was a time when churches would open their doors as a safe haven for people that were victimized.

Today, the problem is if there was a child walking home from school and needed a place to go to get away from the drug dealer trying to recruit them, they would be met by a locked church door or a buzzer to get in. Today, if a single mother of three kids needed help paying rent, the church would require her to go through a 60 day application and approval process only to be told that she can receive half the funds should she come up with the remainder. Today, land has become great real estate for sanctuaries with no soup kitchens, food pantries or outreach services. To the same degree, there are countless organizations and communities crying out for the help of True Christians, but Dead Christians have become too busy to serve or make themselves available for anything outside of their church sponsored events.

Jesus speaks on the importance of works in the community in the book of Matthew the 25th chapter. As Jesus is speaking of the final judgment, He makes reference to the fact that those who serve will be the ones rewarded with the righteousness of God. He says in verses 34-46:

> 34"Then the King will say to those on his right, 'Come, you who are blessed by my Father, inherit the Kingdom prepared for you from the creation of the world. 35For I was hungry, and you fed me. I was thirsty, and you gave me a drink. I was a stranger, and you invited me into your home. 36I was naked, and you gave me clothing. I was sick, and you cared for me. I was in prison, and you visited me.' 37"Then these righteous ones will reply, 'Lord, when did we ever see you hungry and feed you? Or thirsty and give you something to drink? 38Or a stranger and show you hospitality? Or naked and give you clothing? 39When did we ever see you sick or in prison and visit you?' 40"And the King will say, 'I tell you the truth, when you did it to one of the least of these my brothers and sisters, you were doing it to me!' 41"Then the King will turn to those on the left and say, 'Away with you, you cursed ones, into the eternal fire prepared for the devil and his demons. 42For I was hungry, and you didn't feed me. I was thirsty, and you didn't give me a drink. 43I was a stranger, and you didn't invite me into your home. I was naked, and you didn't give me clothing. I was sick and in prison, and you didn't visit me.' 44"Then they will reply, 'Lord, when did we ever see you hungry or thirsty or a stranger or naked or sick or in prison, and not help you?' 45"And he will answer, 'I tell you the truth, when you refused to help the least of these my brothers and sisters, you were refusing to help me.' 46"And they will go away into eternal punishment, but the righteous will go into eternal life."

Jesus makes aware to his listeners the importance of doing for others while here on earth. In this text Jesus outlines how Christ followers can lose their identity by losing their will and passion to serve others. We will further explore this text later in this writing, however one of the primary take aways we can note in Jesus' words is the fact that **service to others is also service to Christ Himself.** Jesus wants us to take away from this text that we cannot forget our responsibilities as servants to humanity because one day we will become accountable for our action and non-action.

Jesus also warns in this text that our death to humanity places the nail in the coffin in our death as perceived in the eyes of God.

There will be some who will read the lines of this book and ask the same questions as the audience of Jesus. There will be countless individuals who will make excuses for why they didn't serve. They will look back on their lives and respond to their responsibilities with the answer, "We didn't know it was you God." But as we are prepared to discover, the absence of Christians in the world has been a detriment to the original message of Christ. What I believe Jesus wanted us to know about the final judgement was that there will be no excuses for why we didn't do what Christ challenged us to do. Jesus is laying forth a strong truth in that **whether you are serving God or serving others that you are serving both simultaneously.**

THE ABSENCE OF CHRISTIANS IN COMMUNITY

I believe it is a horrible misrepresentation of Christ's message for Christians to be absent in the community.

Another interesting dynamic about Christianity is the number of people who have completely disassociated from the label of "Christian" all together. Sarah Pulliam Bailey of the Washington Post writes:

> "Christianity is on the decline in America, not just among younger generations or in certain regions of the country but across race, gender, education and geographic barriers. The percentage of adults who describe themselves as Christians dropped by nearly eight percentage points in just seven years to about 71 percent, according to a survey conducted by the Pew Research Center.[2]

At one point in history people were excited to be a part of this community of believers and service minded individuals. There was a moment in time where having a 'spiritual walk/connection' was just as important to someone as their education, health and career. Now when we look out into the world people have the impression that they can do with, or without, religion and spirituality.

To me, this mindset of non-spiritual necessity, is personal suicide. I live with the philosophy, like many True Christians, that **we are spirits, living in a body and possessing a soul.** Unfortunately, there are people in the world who only give attention to the body and the soul with no regard for their spiritual personhood. People who tend to the needs of the body and are controlled by the desires and wishes of the soul. They spend no time, and have no concern, developing the health of their spirit. Jesus encourages us to pay attention to the higher elements of self and not just

---

[2] Baily, Sarah Pulliam. 2015. *Christianity faces sharp decline as Americans are becoming even less affiliated with religion.* May 12. www.washingtonpost.com/news/acts-of-faith/wp/2015/05/12/christianity-faces-sharp-decline-as-americans-are-becoming-even-less-affiliated-with-religion/.

the spirit in the book of Matthew. He says, "^{25}"That is why I tell you not to worry about everyday life—whether you have enough food and drink, or enough clothes to wear. Isn't life more than food, and your body more than clothing?" (Matthew 6:25)

Some religions would call the spirit 'energy' or the 'God self'. My position is that the world is in the condition it's in because humans are satisfied with the mortal. They have become comfortable taking care of the flesh alone and it has warped their consciousness of their spiritual identity. Humanity has become comfortable feeding the flesh. Humanity has become comfortable chasing the dreams, wishes and passions of today with no concern for their eternal footprint in time. We have become so numb to suffering, death and the disparities of humanity that we have accepted life the way it is. This is what separates Dead Christians from the early church. The early church was unhappy with seeing the sufferings of this world and chose to make a difference through their service.

At one point in antiquity it was cool to be a Christian. I remember the WWJD™ (What Would Jesus Do) trend and how people who didn't attend church were sporting this message. There was a time when people bragged about their churches and religious leaders. There was a time in history where Christians were excited about service opportunities. There was a moment when Christians were on the front line for humanitarian issues. Nonetheless what we have noticed over time is the unfortunate fact that even liars who want to feel like they belong to the "in crowd" won't describe themselves as Christians. People have become so comfortable with being of no religious affiliation at all that even the pretend Christians are disappearing.

Baily writes, "What we're seeing now is that the share of people who say religion is important to them is declining."[3] The fact that people see spirituality as non-relevant to their existence is worrisome. I believe the primary reason for this shift of religious importance is directly connected to the Christian's involvement with humanity. A thing will never be important to an individual if it has no value or significance to the individual. Again, I believe the Christian has died from a server case of non-relevancy. Years ago I came to the realization as to why people 'join' churches. Some of the benefits to joining a community of believers are self-serving within themselves. A member receives free counseling from their Pastor. In the event you chose to get married, you can get free wedding services from your Pastor. I have discovered the ultimate perk to church membership is that when you die you won't have to pay to rent the church out for your service or feed your family after your memorial.

Please don't misinterpret my statement to say that all people join churches for selfish reasons. But when was the last time you heard of a ministry that prided themselves for bringing people back to God for the purpose of service? I have come to observe that many church goers have no idea as to why they joined their church. Many will tell you of the sermon they heard that caused them to move. Others will say that they have always been a member of some fellowship in order to complete a sense of belonging. Some people just want to be able to say that they belong to an organization that is bigger than themselves. I believe when a person chooses to connect with a specific religious group it should be for a greater cause. I believe that when a person decides on a ministry to claim they should have a clear reasoning as to why they want to be a part. Most churches and Pastors echo that membership, and a

---

[3] Baily, Sarah Pulliam. 2015. *Christianity faces sharp decline as Americans are becoming even less affiliated with religion.* May 12. www.washingtonpost.com/news/acts-of-faith/wp/2015/05/12/christianity-faces-sharp-decline-as-americans-are-becoming-even-less-affiliated-with-religion/.

connection, to a church body is in the will of God. Unfortunately, they don't stress the importance of Christian service as the motivator for membership.

Miguel De La Torre writes that, "Regardless of how many different ways the biblical text can be interpreted, certain recurring themes, specifically a call to justice and a call to love, can be recognized by all who call themselves Christians."[4] In other words, it matters not your denomination, your biblical exegesis, your biblical interpretation, your views on the underlining themes of Christianity and its dogmatic orthodox practices if you forget the original message of Christ. There are many seekers of enlightenment who are in desperate need of this message. However, the true message of Christ has become clouded by personal, self-serving agendas that only seek to serve a selected few. If Christians are truly going to be the body of Christ we must take the parts we've been given and put them to work. If God has called you to be a hand in the community then be that hand. If God has called you to be the lung in an environment then be that lung. If God has challenged you to be the brain of change then be that brain. We can no longer expect people to join our churches and fellowships on "God said" alone. The millennial is looking for the answer to "God said for me to what?". This shift in focus, in my opinion, will compel people to come home and connect with their creator.

Clyde Kilough writes for lifehopeandtruth.com. He published a very interesting page answering the question, "Why is Christianity becoming irrelevant?". One of the major points he makes in his writing is how Christianity today looks nothing like what, I believe, Jesus intended for it to look like. I have always pondered

---

[4] Torre, Miguel A De La. 2004. *Doing Christian Ethics from the Margins.* Maryknoll: Orbis Books.

the question in my own ministry that, "If Jesus were alive today would He recognize the Christian movement that was started over 2000 years ago?"[5]

I also ask the question of myself and my ministry, "Would Jesus attend my church? Would Jesus be involved in the things we are doing?" I believe, if Jesus were alive today, that He wouldn't want to just attend church. He would want to be an active participant in the community. Would He see us serving, caring, loving and giving? Or would Jesus be unable to recognize the movement He started because it has been enclosed by largely erected sanctuaries used solely for the purpose of worship and not for outreach? In my opinion the church universal resembles very few characteristics made evident in the early writings of those who pioneered the faith.

Many people are searching for God's presence in the community. Many people are looking for evidence that the spirit of Christ is still alive today. Countless individuals are in search of hope and in desperate need of unconditional love on display. Gandhi says "I am endeavoring to see God through service to humanity, for I know that God is neither in heaven, nor down below, but in everyone."[6] Even Gandhi points us in the consciousness that the kingdom of God will make itself manifest through us. People don't want to hear that God is an away God who "sits high and looks low" on humanity. People don't want to know that God is in heaven judging their every move and motive. People don't want to hear that God isn't pleased with their lifestyle and wants them to change.

What people want to hear is that God loves them the way God created them. People want to hear that God is concerned about their wellbeing. People want to hear

---

[5] Kilough, Clyde. 2015. *Why is Christianity Becoming Irrelevant?* http://lifehopeandtruth.com/change/the-church/why-is-christianity-becoming-irrelevant/.

[6] Kripalani, Krishna. 2004. *Mahatma Gandhi: All Men Are Brothers Autobiographical Reflections.* New York: The Continuum International Publishing Group.

that God is present in the world. I believe that Gandhi was up to something in his statement. What Gandhi observed in his environment was that everyone has a piece of the divine in them. But most importantly people want to know and find comfort with the fact that the divine is with them.

So often do we preach this promise of God to our communities. In the book of Matthew the 28th chapter and the 20th verse Jesus provides a few very comforting words to his disciples.

"Teach these new disciples to obey all the commands I have given you. And be sure of this: I am with you always, even to the end of the age."

What we must note in His statement is the precursor to His promise. That fact that Jesus gave us commandments on how to act and serve humanity cannot be overlooked. We will explore a few of these commandments, along with the greatest commandment, later in this text, however, Jesus encourages us to allow our works to do the talking for us. Jesus is pushing us to understand that in following His commands we guarantee His presence and existence on earth. What we must challenge ourselves to do is to share in the burden of letting the world know that God is with humanity, and will be with humanity, until the end of time. Gandhi says:

> "It is better to allow our lives to speak for us than our words. God did not bear the Cross only 1,900 years ago, but He bears it today, and He dies and is resurrected from day to day. It would be poor comfort to the world if it had to depend upon a historical God who died 2000 years ago. Do not then preach the God of history, but show Him as He lives today through you."[7]

Jesus' presence in the community should not have died the day he ascended to the heavens. Jesus' presence should not have disappeared the day his physical body

---

[7] Kripalani, Krishna. 2004. *Mahatma Gandhi: All Men Are Brothers Autobiographical Reflections.* New York: The Continuum International Publishing Group.

left this earthly world. Rather, when Jesus breathed His spirit on the apostles, there should have been a passing of the service baton. What Matthew 28:20 indicates to us is that each disciple was to teach and be an example to the next generation of disciples.

To place this text in context, Jesus had just raised from the dead. Earlier in the chapter we find the familiar narrative of an empty tomb discovery. What I find noteworthy about this passage is that Jesus doesn't focus on the fact that He had come back from the dead. Rather Jesus reminds his followers of the message he left before his death. There are many Christians who are still in awe of the resurrection of Christ. But we cannot allow this one miraculous event to blind us of the original missive of Christ. We cannot become fixated on the resurrection of Jesus to the point where we make this event our only gospel. Yes, the good news of Christ involves His resurrection. Nonetheless, Jesus also encourages us to echo the news that He would be with us. He promised he would be with the homeless. He would be with the person living with HIV. He would be with the single parent, the felon and the person experiencing domestic violence. He promised that he would be with the prostitute and the person who is hungry or doesn't have clean running water in their village. Jesus didn't just promise that He would raise from the dead, He also promised that He would bring life to our dead situations.

HOW MODERN DAY CHRISTIANS COMPARE TO THE ORIGINAL BELIEVERS?

If the first Christians stood face-to-face with present day Christians what would that faceoff look like?

We cannot negate the fact that Christianity has evolved over history. We must take into consideration that generations have had influences on the identity of Christianity as a religious practice. While the message of Christ has remained the same, its delivery and its significance has been on a cycle of decline and rebirth. We have to accept the fact that today's Christians differ very much from first generation Christians. In the days of Jesus and the early apostles there were no denominations and fellowships. There were no choir robes or praise teams. At its inception there were no Pastors or Bishops. When you think about it there wasn't even a New Testament to read in the early days of Christianity. So how did we produce what we have come to know as Christianity today? And how have these complications and configurations to the faith altered the relevancy of the original message of Christ? Clyde Kilough writes in an article entitled *"Why Christianity is Becoming Irrelevant"* and states*:*

> "We've been doing the same ever since. Christianity came on the scene; but from its inception, people quickly started altering nearly everything about it. For humans to try to "improve" on God is not only arrogant and presumptuous, it also renders our religions irrelevant. The legitimacy of Christianity is totally dependent on whether its creator-Jesus the Christ, who was God on earth-is involved and active in it. If He isn't, it's irrelevant."[8]

Have we lost Jesus in our attempt to showcase His message? Have we strayed away from the greatest commandment with our attempts to make the commandments accessible to others? I agree with Clyde's observation. We have done a great job

---

[8] Kilough, Clyde. 2015. *Why is Christianity Becoming Irrelevant?* http://lifehopeandtruth.com/change/the-church/why-is-christianity-becoming-irrelevant/.

pushing for the advancement and improvement of the worship experience for people. But then again, what have Christians done to make it easier for people to connect and serve the needs of humanity. There are countless things the church has done in order to make coming together convenient and exciting. What tends to perplex the millennial Christian is how hard it's become to get involved and serve. What perplexes the millennial worshipper is the scarcity of opportunities to be of service. The church I pastor in Atlanta, The Worship Center, has experienced exponential growth because of the people who come to us and say, 'my old church made it too difficult to get involved' or 'my old church wasn't doing half the projects you all are involved in'. Because we have kept the message and the practice simple, people have chosen to connect with our ministry in exponential numbers.

The truth of the matter is what started as a movement and a model for service to humanity has become a self-serving machine for religious preservation.

Clyde simplifies his statement by saying, "If Christianity isn't changing people, it isn't relevant."[9] I would like to add to his statement that if Christianity isn't birthing change agents it will become irrelevant.

I still find it amazing at the masses of people who attend church on Sunday morning for hours at a time, but leave with no sense of moral responsibility to change the communities in which they live, learn and lead. It is a sad state of affair at the number of people who claim to be Christian but never experience the transfer of grace that God has made available to them. I am sure it breaks the heart of God to see people refuse to identify themselves as Christ followers when they are involved in community projects. It must be noted the increased level of corporate involvement in our communities because church involvement is at an all-time low. No longer do

---

[9] Kilough, Clyde. 2015. *Why is Christianity Becoming Irrelevant?* http://lifehopeandtruth.com/change/the-church/why-is-christianity-becoming-irrelevant/.

we see church vans unloading in opportunity areas. What we now see are t-shirts marked with corporate logos taking the place of the church.

What consistent action does your church have in the community? But more importantly, what are you, if you identify as Christian, doing consistently to make your mark on the moral compass of humanity?

In comparison with the original Christians, who had no bible like we have today, modern Christians have become extremely dependent on the book as religious text and not as an instruction manual. If we are going to follow the word of God we must be able to make it applicable to our lives. In order for us to apply the text, it must be able to meet our present needs. Gandhi says that scriptures cannot transcend reason and truth. They are intended to purify reason and illuminate truth.[10] We should be using the word of God to find our personal enlightenment regarding the issues that plague humanity. We should embrace the biblical themes of love, hope, grace and service then utilize these universal ideas to guide our hearts and control our actions. The word of God should help us to filter our intentions and motives against the will of God. If we are feeling a push in the direction of service to others, the word of God should validate where our aims derive.

If we are not using God's word in the original intent it was created, we only become hypocrites of the faith. Modern millennials will use this term to describe what the church and Christianity has become today. In their eyes we have strayed from the original message and purpose of Christ. In their eyes we have taken truth and modeled it into our own interpretation of the gospel. Yet there are those who will use the word of God to minimize humanity. My college professor, and now colleague, Dean Dr. Lawrence E. Cater of Morehouse College, and his co-authors of *"Global Ethical*

---

[10] Kripalani, Krishna. 2004. *Mahatma Gandhi: All Men Are Brothers Autobiographical Reflections.* New York: The Continuum International Publishing Group.

Options" provides for us a deeper definition of this word. They write, "Derived from the Greek hypo (under) and krinesthai (to contend), hypocrisy means "to play a part" or "to feign or pretend." The greater the gap between ethical intentions and practice, the greater the hypocrisy.[11] In simpler terms, you shouldn't fake Christianity. We can mean to do well as a Christians and still hurt the brand, which we will discuss later in this text, of the faith. What people should see in our communities is the manifestation of God's word here on earth.

Dean Carter further writes that, Hypocrites are more interested in public relations than in personal accountability. Hypocrites want to be seen in the company of saints, philanthropists, and humanitarians and accumulate honors attesting to their goodness.[12] Paul, in the first chapter of Galatians echoes this sentiment of humility when he writes: *[10]Obviously, I'm not trying to win the approval of people, but of God. If pleasing people were my goal, I would not be Christ's servant.* Both, Dr. Carter and the Apostle Paul, understand that to hold the title of Christian is to also do the work of Christ. We cannot just hang out with other Christians for the sake of being with like-minded people. We cannot do Christian service for the purpose of getting our weekly Christian card stamped. **We cannot be seen wearing the hat of a Christian if our brows do not sweat from the service of Christianity.**

Even Jesus offers a powerful critique of the hypocrites of His time. Jesus saw that the actions of those who professed Judaism did not line up with the message of love and grace that was outlined in the Torah. Jesus points out that those who seek to adorn themselves with religious law and dogma have separated themselves from the will of God. As Jesus says of the hypocrites of his day, the Pharisees: "Now you

---

[11] Carter, Lawrence Edward, George David Miller, and Neelakanta Radhakrishnan. 2001. *Global Ethical Options*. Trumbull: Weatherhill.

[12] Carter, Lawrence Edward, George David Miller, and Neelakanta Radhakrishnan. 2001. *Global Ethical Options*. Trumbull: Weatherhill.

Pharisees make the outside of the cup clean, but your inward part is full of greed and wickedness" (Luke 11:39)[13] Jesus is saying that a person can look the part and still be just as unclean as the ones they condemn. If we are going to return to the model of the early Christians we must be certain that our motives are pure and Christ centered.

We cannot continue building huge and beautiful sanctuaries while girls in our audiences are being sex trafficked and exploited. We cannot continue having church and pastor's anniversaries when there are people still living in homeless situations. We cannot continue beautifying church gardens when there are communities who lack clean running water and suitable soil to grow vegetation. We cannot continue to seek a position to fill on the church's worship program if we are unwilling to fill the voids present in our community.

If we are going to model the original Christian church we must be willing to be a part of the culture that is located in the communities we have been challenged to serve. As we will discover later in this text, the church found in the book of Acts was a true community church. They understood the needs of others and worked collectively to ensure that no one was ostracized. They embraced the culture and views of society and made the gospel shed light on their experiences. In Roger Haight's book, "The Established Church as Mission", he speaks on the fact that interculturation makes new demands: "If the church is to be really immersed in a culture because it grows out of the lived experience of Christ in that culture, then there must be doctrine in new languages, sacramental symbols with new meanings and nuances, church polity with different styles of organization."[14] Only an

---

[13] Carter, Lawrence Edward, George David Miller, and Neelakanta Radhakrishnan. 2001. *Global Ethical Options*. Trumbull: Weatherhill.

[14] Haight, Roger D. 1979. "The 'Established' Church as Mission: The Relation of the Church to the Modern World." *The Jurist 39* (The Jurist #() 11-19.

inculturated church can bear witness to Christ adequately. In other words the gospel message, or the good news, must be relevant to today's news.

Mary Boys, in her book "Educating in Faith" lets us know that the church has a responsibility to name God's activity in the world, to be a prophetic critic of society, and to be a mediating agency, supporting whatever seems to be the manifestation of God's gracious activity in the world.[15] Her words place us on the path to redemption for the Christian faith. Ms. Boys says that we should be pointing out places in society where God's presence can be seen and felt. As Christians we should be able to identify the activities of God in humanity; with the understanding that God is still working in the world. As we look out into the world, we should do as those did in the days of Jesus. We should offer a strong critique on the condition of humanity. Instead of us being critics of one another, we should be placing the injustices of the world under the lens of God's law and order. True Christians should be serving as the midwives to birth change in the world. We should be assisting humanity in its rebirth and revitalization. As those in the early church, we should have a "whatever it takes" mentality to our approach in helping and supporting others.

---

[15] Boys, Mary C. 1989. *Educating in Faith.* Lima: Academic Renewal Press.

WHY AREN'T CHRISTIANS INVOLVED IN THE CHURCH AND COMMUNITY?

Ed Stetzer of *Christianity Today* keeps it simplistic by giving us three reasons Christians are not involved in the church or community:[16]

1. ***"Some people feel useless."*** These individuals feel as if they do not have anything significant to offer in ministry. One interesting dynamic of the church is that many Christians feel as though they have nothing to bring to the table because everything is already being done. It would be thought-provoking to question how many Christians desire service opportunities but find it difficult to plug in without attending a meeting, or class as a prerequisite to serve?

2. ***"Some people are hurting."*** The truth is Christians have been hurt by other Christians and churches. Because of their past, Christians have become hesitant about getting involved again. The heartbeat of God has stopped beating because each day a member of the body at large is being damaged by other members. How can a Christian be expected to serve when those they are serving with don't show the individual how valued they are to the whole? Hurt people hurt other people. However, at some point there has to be the conscious decision to heal the body as a whole.

3. ***"Some people are lazy."*** Let's just be honest. Christianity is, in my personal opinion, the easiest religion to claim and be a part of. Let's also be honest with the fact that some people just don't want to serve. Some Christians would rather be objects of the faith and not partners in the movement of ethical service. Christianity is, in my view, one of the only religions you can profess with no necessary display of devotion.

There are various types of Christians that populate the world: The weak Christian, The non-relevant Christian, The Dead Christian. What they ultimately

---

[16] Stetzer, Ed. 2014. *3 Reasons People are not Involved in Your Church.* June. http://www.christianitytoday.com/edstetzer/2014/june/3-reasons-people-are-not-involved-in-your-church.html.

equate to is the silent heartbeat of God on earth. The truth is that the Christian faith is on the decay. People have stopped believing in the message of Christ because people have stopped seeing the work of Christ being manifested in the world. Christians have become a passive community that would rather respond to a call of action instead of being the leaders who call for change. Dead Christians would prefer to wait until they are needed, instead of finding those communities that need them most. Some Christians will wait until a situation has gone from bad to worse before they give any attention to it. Some Christians will delay until it is a fad to serve. Some Christians will wait until the commercials air before they chose to become involved. One can observe that Christians are not in the community because they chose not to be.

The relevancy of Christianity has been trumped by the irrelevancy of Christian's desire to aid in the inequalities present in society. Christian's unwillingness to serve, in my opinion, functions as a silencer to Christ's message. If faith is on the decline, so is the wellbeing of humanity. If moral change agents remain silent to the issues of the marginalized, hope for humanity is dismal. On the other hand there is hope for this faith; but it can only come when Christians become conscious of their assignment to be the hands, feet and heartbeat of God here on earth. We have to bring awareness of our responsibility to community back to the faith. We have to educate in faith. But most importantly there has to be a desire from Christians to want to do the work of Christ.

I am on the side of Ed in that most Christians have just become lazy. They have lost the fire and the motivation for service. Many Christians have lost the passion for reaching the lost. Many Christians have become comfortable with the blessings of God insomuch that they have forgotten the importance of blessing others. Henri Nouwen, in his book *The Wounded Healer* says, most of us see such an abundance of material commodities around us that scarcity no longer motivates our lives, but at the same time we are groping for direction and asking for meaning and purpose. The future of humanity has now become an option.[17] It is possible to be too blessed? Is it possible that the Grace bestowed to Christians has created a comfortability amongst believers? We have been given such an abundance of God's love that we should be eager to extend that love to others. In the book Matthew of 10th chapter and the 8th verse Jesus encourages us to give as freely as we have received. If we are in search for direction, meaning and purpose we will always find it in our gifts and service to others.

---

[17] Nouwen, Henri J. M. 1972. *The Wounded Healer: Ministry in Contemporary Society.* New York: Doubleday Religion.

WHAT ARE THE ISSUES FACING HUMANITY TODAY?

If Christians Weren't Dead, why are
Humanitarian Issues still Alive?

There is proof to suggest Christians have croaked. Outside of what was mentioned in the previous chapter, there are other proofs to suggest the presence of Christians in the scope of humanity is waning. One could attempt to prove the opposite, however the below mentioned items are on the rise; suggesting the presence of help and hope is dwindling.

My opinion is if True Christians were out doing the work of Christ we would see a drop in the issues that infect civilization. Instead, what we notice in the scope of society is the commonness of social issues. What can be observed, is the largely growing population of the marginalized. What we see happening in the world is a large divide between the church and the community; religion and humanity; salvation and society. There are some cultures who believe in the pairing of opposites. Some may be familiar with the Ying-and Yang of life. If we were to use this same conception with Christianity and humanity, when one sees a global disparity one should also see a True Christian. In the same way opposites attract, Christians should be drawn to the humanitarian issues of the world.

With the availability of resources, technology, and travel there is no excuse for why current social, economic and global issues are still as prevalent as they are. As I have stated before, Christians have access to an abundance of resources and grace. It is interesting to isolate that the below mentioned issues all have simple solutions. If Christians chose to be a part of the solution, their involvement could eradicate much of these, still widespread, problems. In the following pages we will highlight a few specific social and humanitarian issues. We will also, with the help of God's word and fellow critics of the faith, bring enlightenment as it regards to remedying these problems. Many Dead Christians have the perception that a person needs multiple resources, a huge budget and a huge team to make a difference in humanity. The truth is that all a person needs is the willingness to serve and give from what God has blessed them with. What we should understand is that we have more than what we need to make a difference and impact in the global community.

I believe organized religion is to blame as well. There are two things I find problematic with the church: 1. Most people who seek to serve must be a member to participate in functions and 2. Persons are required to go through 'validation hurdles' to serve. The fact that some churches have criteria to participate in service opportunities breaks my heart as a religious leader. There are some organized religious communities that require members to go through orientation and new member's classes before a person can get involved. The last time I checked, when there was a need in the biblical community, people banded together in that moment and handled it. There was no preset criteria that a person had to endure in order to serve. When a problem presented itself those who were willing to serve were on the front line; no questions asked.

Some religious communities and leaders have made it all too hard to get involved and serve. This is one reason I believe people have launched individual initiatives to give back to their communities. This is the reason the college group will make peanut butter and jelly sandwiches on their own to give to the homeless. This is the reason why fraternities and sororities will launch their own clothing drives to donate to women transitioning from domestic violence environments. This is the cause that people will gather their families together to run races, and marathons, to end poverty around the world; because the church and Christians have quit the race.

I would like to present to you a little food for thought: According to USATODAY.com, in an article written by Katherine Muniz, "20 Ways Americans are Blowing their Money", Americans who regularly buy coffee throughout the week spend on average, $1,092 on coffee annually. Yet it costs less than this dollar amount to provide water purification straws to a village in South America who still does not have the technology for clean water. This dollar amount would provide 54 people in a developing country drinkable water. Where are the Christians who drink coffee?

It should pain a Christian's heart to see these issues still exist in the world. We should be uncomfortable with the truths we are ready to uncover in this text. At the same time, it should disgust all human beings to look in the mirror and call themselves 'person' and do nothing about changing these statistics. Numbers don't lie. Research is designed to shed light on ambiguous assumptions. This portion of the text is designed to make people aware of the issues they have chosen to ignore, or turn a blind eye to. The issues listed below should not only serve as statistics and data; nonetheless it should prick our hearts and make us uncomfortable. Discovering these truths should make us sit in our church pews differently. These shocking revelations should make us rethink if we are going to plan the Pastor's next anniversary or send a team to Ghana to build a clean water system?

The goal of this text is not to spark anger or guilt. The goal of the text is to offer a powerful critique on the work of Christians. But ultimately I seek to spark a level of compassion and love within you that will motivate you to act as an agent of love for God. This, I believe, is the message that Christ was pushing us towards. That we should be a community that displays compassion on other communities. Paul writes to the Colossian church, [12]Since God chose you to be the holy people he loves, you must clothe yourselves with tenderhearted mercy, kindness, humility, gentleness, and patience. (Colossians 3:12) Paul echoes the same sentiments of Christ. He reminds us that we have been chosen by Christ for the purpose of displaying Christ's love on others. Compassion and benevolence should be at the root of our Christian existence. We should understand that the communities we have been called to serve were once home for many of us. If it were not for the saving grace of God, many Christians would still find themselves in the hands of the world and on the side of sin and oppression.

Therefore, we should view others in the same regard that we view ourselves. Gandhi says, "whenever I see an erring man, I say to myself I have also erred; when I see a lustful man I say to myself, so was I once; and in this way I feel kinship with everyone in the world and feel that I cannot be happy without the humblest of us being happy.[18] No one is perfect. As we will discuss later in this text, to look in the eyes of the marginalized is to look into our own eyes. We have all sinned and fallen short of the grace of God. Who are we to judge someone else's identity or environment as it relates to our newly graced identity. Instead we should feel a sense of compassion that makes us move in the direction of establishing connections. We should push ourselves to the level where the happiness of others becomes our Christian responsibility. But more importantly, the autonomous value and nature of others should be our primary concern to champion.

---

[18] Kripalani, Krishna. 2004. *Mahatma Gandhi: All Men Are Brothers Autobiographical Reflections.* New York: The Continuum International Publishing Group.

HOMELESSNESS

Homelessness is a social and economic issue that is very near and dear to my heart. Why? Because in 2006 I received an eviction notice on my apartment door that left me in a vicarious situation. I had no money to pay the past month's rent. I had exhausted all of my options for housing and this was the end of the road for me. I had no other option but to begin living out of the rear of my 1998 Chevy Blazer.

I conducted a research assignment while I was getting my Master of Divinity degree at the Interdenominational Theological Seminary. In this assignment I revisited this demographic of people of whom I was once a part of. My discoveries were astonishing! The homeless population in Atlanta is growing. My further research revealed that Atlanta isn't the only metropolitan city that is experiencing a growth in this community of people. The number of people, nationwide, that are finding it hard to keep a roof over their heads is expanding. It already pains my heart that our government's only attempt to address the issue is to disburse the population. However, it is even more painful at the number of Christians and churches that have turned a blind eye to this group. With the exception of Thanksgiving and Christmas, the homeless populations around the nation go unnoticed for a large majority of the year. We see many clothing and food drives which take place during the holiday season, but what work is done throughout the year? How is this specific community receiving support from the religious community in the "off season" of service?

There is a very subtle dynamic as to how people, including Christians, view individuals that are experiencing homelessness. We are aware when they approach our car windows. We are aware when we read the, sometimes humorous, signs held at the intersection. We are aware they sleep under bridges and in business corridors. We are aware they sleep on the front steps of churches. We are aware that there are women and children on the streets of our cities. We are aware of "Tent Cities" around our neighborhoods and urban areas. We are aware that abandoned buildings aren't really abandoned. However, many of us chose to make the person on the opposite side of our visibility equally invisible. We make the conscious choice to ignore what is right in front of our eyes. We are quick to pass judgement without providing any remedy or solution. We have become anxious to do what is convenient, but refuse to stare the issue in the eye and ask the question "What can I do?"

We drive by the homeless on our way to work and school. Although we consciously see them, some of us have been guilty of looking straight through them. It is a sad state of affair but many people, including Christians have made the decision to just ignore the homeless when they "see" them. There is a majority of people who are comfortable with the idea that there will always be homeless people in our cities. Many have become comfortable with the holiday giving campaigns and continued absence throughout the calendar year. Here in Atlanta, in the year 2016, it was projected that over 300 homeless persons would be displaced by the closure of two major shelters in the downtown area. Do you think the Christians have done anything about the closing of these city shelters?

George Boff gives us a perspective to consider when identifying the homeless and the poor in his book *The Bible, The Church and The Poor:*

> The poor are understood as those deprived of the basic necessities to live a life of dignity. According to Clodovis Boff and George Pixley, the poor consist of three distinct groups: 1) the socio-economic poor, consisting of those outside the prevailing economic order (the unemployed, beggars, abandoned children, outcasts, prostitutes) and the exploited (industrial workers paid substandard wages, rural workers, seasonal wage-earners, tenant farmers); 2) the socio-cultural poor, consisting of blacks, indigenous people, and women; and 3) the new poor of industrial societies, consisting of the physically and mentally handicapped abandoned to the streets of huge cities, along with the unemployed, the homeless, the suicidally

depressed, the elderly dependent on insufficient state pensions, and the young addicted to drugs.[19]

We can no longer assume that all people who are poor are substance abusers or mentally challenged veterans. The face, and identity, of the homeless population has broaden in scoop along with the expansion of society. There are countless classes and identities of people who are slowly making their way into association with the homeless community. People experiencing homelessness are often ignored. This is a result of our ignorant assumptions made regarding the condition of the person as well as their intent for help. Many people automatically assume that homeless persons are either: ex-convicts, mental challenged, or substance abusers. Although some of these stereotypes have proven true, there are others on the streets who were, just like many of us, just one paycheck or life event away from losing housing. Another factor is that the cost of living continues to rise in various parts of the country, while wages stays the same. Housing has become so unaffordable for many people that roommate situations, even for professional adults, is on the rise.

If you would like to test this theory you can visit any housing website to see what the average rate of rent is. Multiple that number by three, the common income requirement for consideration, then divide your findings monthly to discover what people in your area need to make in order to afford the housing that is offered. Because I like simple math, a $1000 rental rate can only be afforded by a person who works 40 hours and makes $18.75 per hour (post taxes). This rate, especially in metropolitan cities like Atlanta, isn't even in the "good area" of town. There are some low income areas where people are struggling to pay the average $600 per month in rent. This is completely understandable when the same population is only making $8 an hour.

---

[19] Boff, George V. Pixley & Clodovis. 1989. *The Bible, the Church, and the Poor.* Maryknoll: Orbis Books.

What has the church done? What are Christians going to do in order to help with this matter? What I don't want to do is numb the efforts of those who feed the homeless, have food drives and run soup kitchens during the course of the year. But are we doing enough? Could we be doing more? And are we thinking through our efforts to help this growing population and to prevent economic disparity? These are the serious questions I believe we need to ask the person in the mirror. I also believe there needs to be dialogue and conversation initiated between faith leaders, political influencers and the homeless population. We should all be seated at the same table with the same common goal: to eradicate homelessness.

I have to note that "homeless" people NEED homes and not just food. Otherwise, if food is the only resource we are willing to provide, we should label them as "hungry" people. There are various needs for people living without homes. Shelter, food, healthcare, spiritual support, job placement and countless other human necessities.

I believe there needs to be a call to action in order to address the underline issue: the lack of affordable housing for individuals who live at, or below, the poverty line. There has to be a strategic approach to how we combat this very serious topic. This may sound cruel, but I often laugh at churches and ministries who give food baskets to the homeless population. It's not the basket that is humorous to me, but rather the contents of the package.

Why would you give a homeless person a raw turkey or canned goods when they don't have a stove to prepare them?

What we should be brainstorming are logical solutions to address the issues at their core. We should not seek to pacify the issue. We should not seek solutions that are solely comfortable for us. We should not be willing to do what is convenient for us alone. As Malcolm X reminds us, "What is logical to the oppressor isn't logical to the oppressed. And what is reason to the oppressor isn't reason to the oppressed."[20] With that being said we should be placing ourselves in the shoes and in the minds of those we have been challenged to serve. You would be surprised at the seemingly crazy resources we have at our disposal that are highly coveted in throughout the homeless population. While we utilize socks for our feet, the homeless uses them as hand warmers and carrying purses. We cannot keep doing things for this community that only make sense to us.

To me, there are various gestures we do for the homeless that make absolutely no sense. Again, the matter of homelessness is the absence of affordable housing amongst other necessities. The question to our religious and political leaders is "how can we begin to remedy this problem?" The True Christian's approach to social issues should address the core of what's being presented. Modern Christians have bandaged diseases and diagnosed wounds. Some of our actions are completely backwards. We should be challenging our initiatives and expanding our resources to bridge this economic divide before the world dies on us.

The response is simple. Find affordable housing solutions. I think most Christians believe it is a huge undertaking to provide a homeless person with a home. The truth is that our idea of a home, 3 bedrooms, two bathrooms, a kitchen and a driveway, has clouded our understanding of basic necessities. People need four walls, a roof and basic utilities.

What if we simplified our efforts and provided simple and affordable housing for people living below the poverty line? Tiny houses could be an option. For those

---

[20] X, Malcolm. 1968. *"The Leverett House Forum of March 18, 1964." In The Speeches of Malcolm X at Harvard.* New York: William Morrow & Company.

of us who went to college, and lived in dorms, we should know firsthand that a room with a window is more than enough to get through life.

While the homeless population in on the rise in some areas of the country it is not unfathomable for Christians to come together in order to provide inexpensive and modest housing to this demographic. If our ministries and organizations can raise the capital to build multi-million dollar facilities we can definitely raise a few thousand dollars to erect individual living quarters for those who are living out on the streets. If we can occupy acres of land in order to build community development centers, we can add on a few acres of frontage to place small communities of tiny homes.

It is not my intent to get rid of effective feeding programs. I do not want people to stop hitting the streets to serve. I do not want those who do clothing drives to cease their campaigns. Nevertheless we cannot turn a blind eye to the root issue of HOMElessness. With the quantity of abandoned buildings and vacant, government owned, real estate, there is no excuse to the numbers of people who still have no place to lay their head at night.

You may not consider it a serious problem in our culture because of the two people you see panhandling on your way to and from work. You may live in an area where there are no signs of homelessness at all. You may see in your community, or state, the homeless population really is invisible or nonexistent. On the other hand, please allow me to shed some light on your perception. "On a single day in January 2014, 578,424 people were experiencing homelessness-meaning they were sleeping outside or in an emergency shelter or transitional housing program."[21] Please keep in mind this does not include the number of people that sleep on couches until they get off their feet; or those who have found refuge in abandoned buildings. These numbers

---

[21] National Alliance to End Homelessness. 2015. *The State of Homelessness in America 2015*. April 1. www.endhomelessness.org/library/entry/the-state-of-homelessness-in-america-2015.

should be mindboggling! Other statistics have suggested that there are well over 1,000,000 Americans who do not have a place to call their own.

I am sure some people would read the number 578,424 and would turn a deaf ear to the situation by stating this statistic is not so bad when there are approximately 320 million people living in the United States. As a Christian, I believe 1 person sleeping on the streets is more than enough to call for action. Christ consciousness, as we will discuss later in this text, doesn't take numbers into consideration. Christ consciousness is concerned with the individual lives that need to be touched. It is a message that provides unique hope and the expectancy of specific grace.

Although the homeless population makes up less than one percent of the national population we have been called to serve the "invisible people". One can assume this perception is why we have seen outreach to this community die. Maybe it is because people don't see it as a 'major' issue. We should be reminded that our call to service is a call to help the least and the lost. If the least and the lost are present in our communities then True Christians should be active in reaching out to them. Until the homeless population gets to 0 True Christians should be relentless in their efforts to eradicate this gap. In the book of Luke the 15th chapter, Jesus stresses the importance of caring for the one (1). His succession of parables talk about the 1 lost sheep, the 1 lost coin, and the 1 lost son. When will we, as Christians, make the conscious decision to go after the one?

I also believe the reason Christians have not shown a huge interest to this community is because we have already predetermined the face of this population. When The Worship Center started feeding the homeless population of Atlanta in 2012 I was shocked and heartbroken at the number of children who would frequent our line on the first Friday of every month. Not only did we begin serving the mouths of persons who looked like working professionals, but the number of mouths that were under the age of 12 was heart breaking. "One quarter of homeless people are children. HUD reports that on any given night, over 138,000 of the homeless in the U. S. are children under the age of 18."[22] The heart of God beats for the children as well.

You will hear me say this a few times throughout the rest of this text, but *if that news didn't break your heart as a Christian you should turn in your Christian card.*

What is problematic with most people, including Christians, is that we only like to address what we see; instead of searching for the environments that need our help and support. When an issue, or cause, is in the headlines we like to rally and support. But what about the silent assassins that are killing our community, society, humanity and the Christian population itself? We have to do better, but we also have to seek the knowledge associated with the environment to help address the issues. I don't just blame ignorant Christians, I also blame uninformed Pastors and leaders who fail at the quest for humanitarian enlightenment. We can't blame people for not knowing when Pastors only focus self-serving agendas. Just because we don't see it on a day to day basis does not mean it is undeserving of our attention. Just because we turn on the television and never cross a commercial or headline to address this economic disparity does not mean we should not be drawn to champion its remedy.

Gandhi says we should be ashamed of resting or having a square meal so long as there is one able-bodied man or woman without work or food.[23] The reality is that many of us will not lose sleep over this issue, or the other issues presented in this text.

---

[22] Quigley, Bill. 2015. *10 Facts About Homelessness.* January 18. www.economyincrisis.org/content/10-facts-about-homelessness.

[23] Kripalani, Krishna. 2004. *Mahatma Gandhi: All Men Are Brothers Autobiographical Reflections.* New York: The Continuum International Publishing Group.

However, our moral compass should rattle when we see God's children living less than the life of a King's Kid. If we profess that God is our Father and those around us are our siblings, we should be uneased knowing that our nieces and nephews sleep with the rodents of the streets.

How can Christians be led into social and humanitarian change when the leaders are unaware of the problems that need to be addressed?

There are other factors that attribute to homelessness. One factor many Christians chose to remain quite about is domestic violence. We will discuss this issue in a later chapter by itself. However, "Domestic violence is a leading cause of homelessness among women. According to the National Law Center on Homelessness and Poverty (NLCHP), more than 90 percent of homeless women are victims to sever physical or sexual abuse, and escaping that abuse is a leading cause of their homelessness."[24] What we can learn from this discovery is that every social and humanitarian effort is undergirded by a moral issue. If the bible serves as a moral compass, True Christians should be able to get to the root of some of these disparities. As Christians, we should be the champions and advocates for moral change. As I will discuss in the following chapter, human sex trafficking and sexual exploitation will leave a victim homeless as well often times when they make the decision to exit the industry.

The resources are at our disposal. Our hands are able to do the work. Our feet are able to go to the communities that need the most attention. Our voices are able to speak out regarding the government's displacement agendas. If we are able to build buildings to house our worship services, we are able to build homes to house those who can't afford basic housing. Henri Nouwen points out that we are

---

[24] Quigley, Bill. 2015. *10 Facts About Homelessness.* January 18. www.economyincrisis.org/content/10-facts-about-homelessness.

confronted not only with the most elaborate and expensive attempts to save the life of one person by heart transplantation, but also with the powerlessness of the world to help when thousands of people die from lack of food.[25] Poverty is real. The same passion we have to advance technology, education, and government, we should have the same drive to end this disparity. As we are moving the world forward we cannot forget the forgotten. In the same way we are raising awareness for health issues around the world we should also be making aware the social issues and injustices that plague humanity at home.

There are many things happening around us. There are many communities that make up this planet we call earth. There are various paths that people take to find meaning in life. But will all the variables life presents us we should be able to glue together a perspective that gives us purpose. As Henri Nouwen states, People confronted with all this and trying to make sense of it cannot possibly deceive themselves with one idea, concept, or thought system that would bring these contrasting images together into one consistent outlook on life.[26] I would disagree that there is one thing that will bring this chaos called life together: Love for one another.

---

[25] Nouwen, Henri J. M. 1972. *The Wounded Healer: Ministry in Contemporary Society.* New York: Doubleday Religion.

[26] Nouwen, Henri J. M. 1972. *The Wounded Healer: Ministry in Contemporary Society.* New York: Doubleday Religion.

HUMAN SEX TRAFFICKING AND SEXUAL EXPLOITATION

Sex Trafficking is another one of those diminutive issues that churches and Christians are afraid to address. One of the cultural issues Christians still need to address is being comfortable with the word 'sex' in our religious conversations. This three letter word is still heard as a 'dirty' word if said in the context of the church. Heaven forbid a religious leader uses this word from religious podiums. I have come to the conclusion that most Christians are uncomfortable with this expression because their sex lives aren't what they desire! It becomes painful to talk about things individuals still can't get right in their own personal lives. Sex has become a taboo. Not because of the action itself, but because of the connotations we have made surrounding this natural human element.

I heard comedian Steve Harvey remark in one of his standups a few years ago that he doesn't know why the church and Christians are still so afraid of the word sex? He makes the observation: "how do you think all these little baby Christians got here?"

Sex trafficking, pornography, sex enslavement and prostitution were other issues that became near and dear to my heart while I was pursuing my Master of Divinity degree. I was enrolled in an ethics course at the Interdenominational Theological Center when Professor, Dr. Riggins Earl, challenged us engage with any social-ethical dilemma of our choice. While my colleagues were researching 'safe' topics, I made the decision to go deep into the darkness of sexual ethics. What I discovered most about this moral, social and economic business was jaw dropping. Yet Christians are completely unware of what lies beyond the dark shadows of the night. I believe this is because they are comfortable in the light they have found.

If True Christians are going to live up to the title they possess, we are going to have to get comfortable being uncomfortable. We are going to have to be willing to engage with the forbidden. We must be willing to speak up for those who have been silenced because of their condition and not their potential. True Christians can't stay in the safe zone of service. The service model of Jesus does not illustrate a perfect environment to serve. The service model of Jesus does promote actions that only involve orthodox praxis. What the service model of Jesus challenges us to do is to engage with those who the community has labeled as unclean and unworthy of our attention and work.

My personal opinion is if Christians chose to rise up and regain the heartbeat of God, it is going to take us engaging with situations that are literally killing and hurting humanity as a whole. It is going to involve us dialoguing, as Jesus did, with the communities that others refused to acknowledge.

According to CNN, "More than 3,500 sex trafficking cases were reported to the National Human Trafficking Resource Center last year alone."[27] A person must note that these are the *reported* cases. This does not take into account the individuals who are selling others for sexual favors in exchange for compensation or living necessity trades. This does not account for the parent who offers their child for sex in order to keep the landlord from evicting them. This does not take into account the women who willingly enter the cam-to-cam world because her wages are not enough to support her children. This does not mention the people who are coaxed into being recorded exercising sexual acts in exchange for money without knowing their images, and actions, will be placed on the World Wide Web. Government and other organizations have found it difficult to penetrate this world of "Pimps" and "Johns". They have found it hard to pin point who the victims are and who the victimizers are. The loyalty of this community has made it hard to rescue the exploited from the exploiter. These numbers do not included pornography slaves, and those who are

---

[27] Ford, Leif Coorlim and Dana. 2015. *Sex Trafficking: The New American slavery*. July 21. www.cnn.com/2015/07/20/us/sex-trafficking/.

sexually exploited for the gain of another. Sex trafficking, and sexual exploitation, is a multi-billion dollar a year industry and many influential leaders participate in this immoral act of enslavement.

This reality, however, leads to a very staggering point with regards to why this moral issue has not made it to the surface of our moral compass; money. "Some traffickers in Atlanta make more than $32,000 a week. The Study also cited research findings from 2007 that Atlanta's illegal sex industry generates $290 million a year."[28] Not only does sex sell...sex pays. There are many persons, both men and women, who are making huge profits on the backs of others; or should I say, make huge profits while others lay on their backs. The exchange of capital flows through the hands of many in the sex trafficking industry. Meanwhile, the focus of the church remains on self-serving initiatives.

The rate at which this "industry", as they have now labeled it because of its economic nature, is growing has become sickening and alarming. Nevertheless, Christians and churches see no problem. I have to applaud one of our ministry partners who is leading the cause in the metro Atlanta area; The Atlanta Dream Center. They are an organization who actually ministers to all elements of sexual exploitation (not solely sex slaves). My working with them has helped me to redefine the nature of this moral issue. My assumption about sex trafficking was that it only involved those who were being sold in sex slavery. What I have been enlightened to understand is that it also involves those who are forced into pornography, prostitution and exploitation. The smaller communities in this larger issue also need the attention of our churches and Christians. But again, if contemporary Christians don't see the issue, or aren't willing to approach the issue, it will never be a concern.

---

[28] Ford, Leif Coorlim and Dana. 2015. *Sex Trafficking: The New American slavery*. July 21. www.cnn.com/2015/07/20/us/sex-trafficking/.

There are so many criminally associated issues that conservative Christians chose to address without even looking in the direction of human trafficking. But did you know, "Human trafficking is the third largest international crime industry (behind legal drugs and arms trafficking). It reportedly generates a profit of $32 billion every year. Of that number, $15.5 billion is made in industrialized countries."[29] If contemporary Christians can stand up for drugs and gun laws why can't they move one further level in order to change laws that relate to sexual exploitation? More laws need to be put in place that would advocate for women, men, and children being caught in sex crimes to be treated as victims and not as criminals. Every two and four years we see the conservative Christians making their political stands about economic and social issues during the election season. In my short presence here on earth I have never seen human sex trafficking and exploitation brought to the forefront of American politics. This becomes problematic when our international airports and hotels have become hubs and service centers for those who desire sex for money.

We have seen countless places throughout the biblical text, both Old Testament and New Testament, where the personhood and value of an individual was given an economic worth. Whether for a commodity trade or a flat rate currency exchange, sex has been used to satisfy the economic systems of the world. The problem arises when people lose their autonomous value because of the actions they have made in order to satisfy empirical costs.

Yet, as many theologians, such as Enrique Dussel of Mexico, have pointed out, God's reign in community is an affirmation that people are created to live in a positive relation with the Divine and with each other. This cannot happen when individuals are reduced to their economic value, when they become objects or

---

[29] Do Something Organization. n.d. *11 Facts about Human Trafficking.* www.dosomething.org/facts/11-facts-about-human-trafficking.

resources to be exploited.[30] God did not create humanity for the sake of exploitation. God did not give each of individuality only to be demoralized for the sake of lining someone else pockets. I believe when God gave us the ability, and commandment, to work that it was God's intents for us to use our energy to manifest something of value and not to become sexual currency.

---

[30] Dussel, Enrique. 1988. *Ethics and Community Trans. Robert R. Barr.* Maryknoll: Orbis Books.

LACK OF CLEAN WATER IN DEVELOPOING COUNTRIES

Lack of Clean Water across the globe is another issue I believe modern Christians should turn their attention to. "More than 840,000 people die each year from a water related disease."[31] While some country populations get excited about the newest smart phone or the next luxury automobile, there are still developing countries who lack this basic necessity.

Before you begin reading this portion of text I think you should go and get yourself a glass of water.

As a matter of fact, I can probably make a safe assumption that you have bottled water somewhere nearby. And even if you do not, you can still participate in the following exercise. Pour the water in a glass if you will. But before you place your lips to this refreshing goblet of hydration I want you to consider adding a few things to your liquid reciprocal. Let's begin by mixing a few drops of your partner's bath water from last night to your cup. Then we can add a few drips of motor oil from your neighbor's motorcycle outside. Let's also take a ride up the road and see if we can capture some cow urine to give it a bit of flavor and color. As unappetizing as these ingredients my sound to you, there are millions of people in the world who drink waters with these impurities in it daily. They drink the same water others bathe in. They consume the same water people wash their automobiles in. They ingest the same water that catches animal waste.

I am apologetic if my sarcasm made your stomach turn; but I hope you have come to realize there are literally hundreds of millions of people that still do not have access to the simplicity of clean water? For many of us, we have become so comfortable with our life styles to take something so simple for granted. Many of us

---

[31] Water.org. n.d. *Millions Lack Safe Water.* www.water.org/water-crisis/water-facts/water/.

don't just have access to clean water that dispenses from our faucet, we have the options of bottled water and even flavored water. Yet there are hundreds of children, and adults who die each day of dehydration and other water borne illnesses.

To me it is fascinating how some Christians can be so concerned, and will cast judgement, about drinking alcohol, yet remain silent about the absence of clean running water in developing countries. If we can be passionate about the saving the world from drunkardness, surely we can champion a cause that will save the lives of millions by implementing technology that will purify contaminated water.

What pains my heart all the more, and should pain yours as well, are the simple solutions that technology has introduced in order to provide pure drinking water to these populations. There are options at our disposal from water purification straws ($19.95 each), to self-managed water purification systems ($2595.00 for a full system), to fully functioning water wells ($4,000.00 projects). Nonetheless, our churches will spend ten times these amounts on vacation bible school books and Sunday school curriculums. Churches will budget $10,000 a year for church beautification items while families are forced to drink contaminated water. Meanwhile, some Christians will also pledge 4 to 5 times these amounts to building funds, auxiliary dues and Pastoral Anniversary assessments. Some people spend more on their church choir robes and mother's board hats that they do on mission's projects.

When will we redirect our attention to the needs of humanity instead of the wants and desires of self? When will the church stop being selfish and adopt the message of Christ to be selfless?

In The Worship Center's first year of being opened, and with less than 100 weekly attendees, The Worship Center was able to begin two water purification system projects in the Dominican Republic and Ghana. Yet there are surrounding ministries that have multi-million dollar budgets that won't plant 1% of their budget into a project like this. Have Christians, and the church, become so comfortable with our blessings that we have become blind to the opportunities to bless others? The resources modern Christians have access to are immeasurable. Yet much of these resources stay filtered through the walls of the church and never reach the community, or the globe.

Pastors, preachers, and religious leaders will often expound from the text, John 4:14 "but whoever drinks the water I give them will never thirst. Indeed, the water I give them will become in them a spring of water welling up to eternal life." (NIV) Traditional Christians have become so focused on Jesus being the living water and their own "springs of eternal life" to the point where contemporary Christians have become spiritually dehydrated. If we are going to preach this message of hope it will also need to be a relevant message. If we are going to continue utilizing the analogies of the biblical text we must be willing to ensure those analogies remain relevant to contemporary society. There are various places throughout the bible which speak on the living water of Christ or utilize water as an analogy for hope:

> **John 4:14** - But whoever drinks of the water that I will give him will never be thirsty again. The water that I will give him will become in him a spring of water welling up to eternal life."
>
> **John 7:38** - Whoever believes in me, as the Scripture has said, 'Out of his heart will flow rivers of living water.'"
>
> **John 4:13-15** - Jesus said to her, "Everyone who drinks of this water will be thirsty again, but whoever drinks of the water that I will give him will never be thirsty again. The water that I will give him will become in him a spring of water welling up to eternal life." The woman said to him, "Sir, give me this water, so that I will not be thirsty or have to come here to draw water."

Revelation 21:6 - And he said to me, "It is done! I am the Alpha and the Omega, the beginning and the end. To the thirsty I will give from the spring of the water of life without payment.

John 7:37 - On the last day of the feast, the great day, Jesus stood up and cried out, "If anyone thirsts, let him come to me and drink.

John 7:37-39 - On the last day of the feast, the great day, Jesus stood up and cried out, "If anyone thirsts, let him come to me and drink. Whoever believes in me, as the Scripture has said, 'Out of his heart will flow rivers of living water.'" Now this he said about the Spirit, whom those who believed in him were to receive, for as yet the Spirit had not been given, because Jesus was not yet glorified.

A person can go days, and even weeks, without food. However, if a person goes without water for a long duration the body will begin to shut itself down. Not just earth, but our universe has an abundance of water. We have been blessed, and graced, to be on a planet where this life giving resource is at our disposal. If the creation story describes humanity's appointment as stewards of the earthly resources, then as caretakers, human beings are called to protect, preserve, and safeguard those resources so that all can benefit and enjoy their fruits. Creation as gift means that all living creatures have a basic right to its products and no group has the right to hoard its resources.[32] Every child of God has the right to participate in the free flowing resources of our creator. We should have compassion on those who don't have the ability to enjoy a bottle of Dasani™; let alone a village who is unable to filter the water they collect from the local watering hole.

We should be thirsty to serve!

You may be asking, what should modern Christians be doing then? There is another simple solution and answer to this question. I have already listed three

---

[32] Torre, Miguel A De La. 2004. *Doing Christian Ethics from the Margins.* Maryknoll: Orbis Books.

resources available in order to provide relief for this global problem. There are countless, and credible, organizations that have taken the lead in battling this problematic disparity. It is our responsibility as True Christians to find them and support them. In the same regard that we can Google™ "water fountains for church vestibule" we can enter the words "clean water organizations in developing countries".

I would also encourage churches and True Christians to not just send money in order to say "I gave" or "we built" towards the cause. It is easy to throw money at a problem or issue and feel as though a difference has been made based on your financial contribution. To the privileged church, and Christian, we can become comfortable with others doing the work while we write a check. Instead, challenge yourself to actually go and serve. Make it a point to be a hands on Christian. Make it your mission to literally touch humanity. Make the decision to use your "vacation time" at work as "service time". I know there are some people who have accumulated weeks of vacation time at their place of employment. Why not take a week to serve and let your job pay for you to serve? A mission's trip to Ghana to build a water purification system costs less than that trip to Las Vegas you've been planning!

This is the first humanitarian issue, in this text, I believe requires Christians doing a dirty word: missions. This is the issue I believe the American Church can have the greatest impact. While there may be the lack of clean running water in the states, there is a greater need for this living necessity across the oceans. Many traditional Christians have become so comfortable with throwing money at problems that they have lost the desire to be physically active and present in the happenings of hope. True Christians don't mind getting out and getting our hands dirty. It may take sacrificing your 10 day trip to Paris which would cost $3700 to go to the Dominican for $900 and stay with the locals, but the impact made will be priceless.

If we are going to be True Christians of service we must also be willing to be Christians of personal sacrifice.

The numbers are staggering; and these numbers should motivate us to act on this ecological disparity. Approximately "750 million people around the world lack access to safe water; approximately one in nine people."[33] There are still innumerable villages and countries that do not have the technology and resources that many other populations have been fortunate enough to receive. The good news is that modern technology to make clean water accessible to developing countries is mobile and affordable. Years ago the statistic of people who lacked clean, drinkable, water was over 1 billion! Now, because of modern technology, and sourcing, we have been able to lower this sum. However, there is still much work that has to be done. The True Christian's goal, as with the homeless population outlined in the previous chapter, is to diminish this number to 0. With the number of True Christians, and True Churches, in the world we can end this deadly situation regarding a simple commodity.

What is even more heartbreaking is the number of children, and adolescents that have been effected by this global disparity.

> "An estimated 801,000 children younger than 5 years of age perish from diarrhea each year, mostly in developing countries. This amounts to 11% of the 7.6 million deaths of children under the age of five and means that about 2,200 children are dying every day as a result of diarrheal diseases."[34]

Almost one million children die each year as a result of not being able to drink clean water. To see a child drink from a contaminated stream is heart breaking.

---

[33] Water.org. n.d. *Millions Lack Safe Water.* www.water.org/water-crisis/water-facts/water/.

[34] Centers for Disease Control and Prevention. 2015. *Global WASH Fast Facts.* June 5. www.cdc.gov/healthywater/global/wash_statistics.html.

What is sadder is the fact that many of these children have no other choice but to drink from these waters to survive. Taste matters not to them. Since this is the only source of hydration for some communities, children have no option but to drink from the same springs the farm animals drink from. Filtration is their least concern. Because when a person is thirsty anything wet will have to do. A thirsty child needs to drink water; contaminated or otherwise. While some Christians feed their children soft drinks and flavored punch, there are parents who force their children to swallow brown water at birth.

As I stated previously, the American Church should take the lead in this global epidemic. There are few states who lack clean running water, however there are countless countries who are not afforded the same opportunity. When Jesus speaks about reaching the nations, this, I believe, is one of the areas he would have wanted us to address. Gandhi says that there is no limit to extending our services to our neighbors across state-made frontiers. God never made those frontiers.[35] Whether in Maryland, Georgia, California or Idaho, we cannot forget our brothers and sisters in Ethiopia, Chad, Haiti and Ghana. While Christianity may not be prevalent in these communities we cannot forget that to serve humanity, regardless of religious backdrop, is to serve God.

While modern American Christians have the convenience of walking to the refrigerator, or local gas station for water, there are communities of people who have to walk miles in order to gather contaminated water. There are women who carry multiple gallons of non-purified water, on their heads, back to their villages to nurture their children and families. We should look at their sufferings and have compassion for their plight. Gandhi also says:

---

[35] Kripalani, Krishna. 2004. *Mahatma Gandhi: All Men Are Brothers Autobiographical Reflections.* New York: The Continuum International Publishing Group.

"I cannot imagine anything nobler or more national than that for, say, one hour in the day, we should all do the labour that the poor must do, and thus identify ourselves with them and through them with all mankind. I cannot imagine better worship of God than that in His name I should labour for the poor even as they do."[36]

While the literal sense of Ghandi's message would have millions of people walking around the metropolitan streets of the U. S. with pots on their head, we cannot minimize his memorandum of empathy for the quandary of others. If this discovery of lacking clean water in developing countries does not break your heart, or propel you to act on this issue, you have permission to relinquish your "Christian Card".

---

[36] Kripalani, Krishna. 2004. *Mahatma Gandhi: All Men Are Brothers Autobiographical Reflections.* New York: The Continuum International Publishing Group.

DOMESTIC VIOLENCE

Domestic Violence is another one of those hush-hush issues many Christians fall victim to but are too afraid to address publically. There is a large number of women, and men, who attend our churches on Sunday morning with an excessive amount of cosmetics on in order to cover the bruises they incurred at the hands of their partner the night before. Domestic violence is one of those issues many people can sense when they feel as though someone is going through it. Why? Because many of us can identify a person who is afraid or living in fear. I have seen, and been able to pick up first hand, the traits that would identify a person who is in an abusive relationship: When people avoid specific topics they believe will anger their partner. When you observe a partner who is consistently putting down or humiliating their counterpart. When you notice a partner who is excessively jealous or possessive. These are only a few signs that could indicate that a person is experiencing domestic violence.

The general assumption regarding domestic violence involves a young girl who falls in love with an older man who has an anger problem. The reality is the face of domestic violence has changed over the years. The situations that were once norms have now been replaced with new lenses of interpretation. Now we are finding women who have been married for 20 years experiencing this dark character trait of their spouse. We are discovering character transformations where people who were loving and kind decades ago have grown to become violent in their rage. In the same way people change, so does the dynamics of one's relationship with that change. How people handle stress and life events can trigger certain behavioral deviations.

We are not who we were yesterday because we face new stresses and anxieties today. Taking this information into consideration, no person is immune from becoming a victim or a perpetrator. We are all evolving daily. While you may not consider it now, we all have the potential to be a victim of domestic violence or a person who inflicts harm on an individual we profess to love. While we may be accustom to women being the primary victims in this social stigma, the numbers for men who are experiencing an abusive relationship are also on the rise.

Domestic violence is another one of those silent, in home, issues many Christians, evidently, believe should be handled in the privacy of a person's home. Most people believe this issue should be addressed by local authorities and relationship counselors; I beg to differ. In most cases it is not until the victim is permanently disabled, mutated, or killed that we see attention given to these cases. It is not until the church is called to bury the victim that we make the choice to give attention to the issue.

I remember hearing the story of a woman who had experienced domestic violence for years and could never find refuge in her circle of Christian friends. She was in a women's ministry and a small group, but no one was able to hear her cries for help. No one ever asked why her husband never attended these spiritual growth sessions. People assumed he was either uninterested or had to work late. What they did not know what that her church attendance was her only method to escape home. It was something she went through alone because of the embarrassment, and judgement, she knew she would feel if her fellow Christians found out. When she did find the courage to approach her Pastor about her circumstance, his response was for her to "stick it out, get counseling and pray that God would change his heart."

Today she still has fragments of the bullet her husband put in her head; permanently lodged in her skull because removing them would cause damage to the brain.

She was blessed and fortunate to survive this ordeal. But it wasn't until the sound of the gun went off that people heard her voice. There are so many people who suffer in silence at the hands of a partner they love. There are dozens who believe the vows they made, for better or for worse, trump the painful experience they are in. There are those who hope and pray for a change in a person who has no desire to change. There are some who refuse professional help and spiritual counsel. There are multiple individuals that are too afraid to leave, yet too in love to liberate themselves from the hands, and fists, and kicks, and blows of an aggressive loved one. As True Christians, it should sadden our hearts at the number of lives lost each year by this act of misguided anger and passion.

> The current statistics are shocking. Did you know that:
>
> "3 is the number of women murdered every day by a current or former male partner? In the U.S. 38,028,000 is the number of women who have experienced physical intimate partner violence in their lifetimes. 18,500,000 is the number of mental health care visits due to intimate partner violence every year. And 10,000,000 children are exposed to domestic violence every year."[37]

These numbers are too gigantic not to go unnoticed. These numbers deserve the attention of those who have learned what compassion looks like and how unconditional love should be displayed.

Not only are women suffering from the physical abuse of domestic violence, but children are experiencing psychological scars that make them: 1. afraid of the oppressor's personality type as they get older or 2. Puts them at a greater propensity to revisit these same displays of aggression as they mature as victim or aggressor. In other words, children will fear what scared them, or they will reenact and become what frightened them. What they see will be assumed as normative and acceptable. Either way we must be committed to breaking the family curses that are a result of domestic violence. We should be committed to teaching the love of Christ to our

---

[37] Vagianos, Alanna. 2015. *30 Shocking Domestic Violence Statistics that Remins us its an epidemic.* February 13. www.huffingtonpost.com/2014/10/23/domestic-violence-statistics_n_5959776.html.

children. We should be advocates for the type of love that is mentioned in Ephesians 5:25-26, "For husbands, this means love your wives, just as Christ loved the church. He gave up his life for her to make her holy and clean, washed by the cleansing of God's word". While the context of the scripture is referring to a spirit-guided relationship between the husbands and wives of the church of Ephesus, we cannot ignore the foundational root message located in this text: to love others in the same way that God loves us. This message is not solely for married couples. This message is for anyone, and everyone, who is blessed to be in a position to love another.

The argument regarding domestic violence, and the Christian's role as a beacon of hope and support, is that we can't be afraid to initiate dialogue with the victims and the victimizers. Most domestic violence situations require a mediator. Because the issue involves multiple people and personalities it often requires conversation and consideration of, and with, the other. I believe the biggest fear in our churches, and amongst the faith, is the potential of discovering who the aggressors are as well. This discovery won't make the faith look favorable if the aggressors turn out to be influential church leaders or respected parishioners. In multiple situations this proves to be the case. As Christians, our concern, as was Jesus', is that we advocate for justice on behalf of the oppressed. For those who have lost their voice, or are too afraid to speak on their circumstance, we should be listening for their silent cries. We must learn to advocate for those who have lost their say in hopeless environments. We must speak up for those who have been forced into silence.

What needs to first happen is the creation of safe environments where victims can come without judgement or embarrassment. One observation is that some victims are afraid of perception and persecution from the outside. How will I be viewed? What will people think about me? What will people think about my partner? These are the thoughts that pass through the minds of those searching for a way out. Secondly, we cannot be afraid to act on behalf of the victim. Upon discovering the condition of the victim, we must be willing to face the problem head on. This will typically involve facing the person who has done the harm. If nothing else the victim needs support. The victim needs comfort in knowing that they are no longer alone in facing this battle. The person needs to know that their environment, and them as a person, will not be judge for something that was beyond their control.

Domestic violence situations have proven tricky over the years. True Christians must remain delicate to the situation and understand their role to the victim and the aggressor; both should be extended the grace and love of God. Much of this delicacy is due to the level of manipulation, fear and commitment between the couple. These factors make the situation one that cannot be approached lightly. True Christians should be willing to approach the issue with sensitivity, and prayer, while partnering with professionals that can effectively guide the victim through a process of restoration and safety. Simultaneously, the aggressor will need the support necessary to work through their unhealthy behavioral expressions.

The task with this household issue is that it is exactly that: a household issue. In order to get to the root of the problem it would take the community of believers walking through the doors of people's homes instead of peeping through their windows and listening through their walls. Domestic violence, in some instances, does spill into the streets of our communities. But in most cases the violence is perpetrated within the home. Did you know that "Every 9 seconds in the US, a woman is assaulted or beaten? On a typical day, there are more than 20,000 phone calls placed on domestic violence hotlines nationwide. Only 34% of people who are injured by intimate partners receive medical care for their injuries."[38] There is very little reported on the number of men who suffer at the hands of their partner. We have to be willing to destigmatize the perception that only women experience domestic violence. The

---

[38] National Coalition Against Domestic Violence. n.d. *Statistics.* www.ncadv.org/learn/statistics.

modern Christians of the world will never hear these calls or see their bruises because of their refusal to enter the dark world of domestic violence. We cannot be afraid to peel back the curtains of the living rooms, bedrooms and kitchens where anger turns into violence on a consistent basis. These victim's voices will continue to go unheard because traditional Christians would rather hear about the next church meeting.

HIV/AIDS

It's a sensitive topic, but what better people to show compassion than True Christians. The **HIV/AIDS Epidemic** is still a topic most churches and Christians refuse to take a consistent role in. On designated and commemorative days and months the topic is mentioned. However my observation is that there are few churches and ministries that have consistent support, education and awareness regarding this health issue. It amazes me at the current level of ignorance presently displayed by people around this health issue as well. It baffles me at the lies and myths people continue to believe from the early 1980s; where it was believed HIV made its first appearance in the United States. The fact of the matter is churches have not educated their congregations; and Christians have made HIV/AIDS the present day leprosy. As I will later discuss in this chapter, we have created this health issue and made it into a moral issue. Because of this perpetual ignorance and stigmas associated with HIV/AIDS there are countless people literally dying in silence.

I must admit it was not until I was studying for my Master of Divinity degree that I was made aware of the truths associated with this health issue. Here I was, a religious leader for over a decade, with very little knowledge and truth about this virus. I too fell victim to the ignorance associated with this health issue. There were still ideas and words I heard that I had made truth in my experience. Never once did I sit down to research and discover the actual health finds and facts about HIV/AIDS. To this day I remember the plethora of information that I received in one particular class that, originally, I was ignorant to. I remember sitting in class and saying to myself, "Wendel you have to do better". I remember saying to myself, "Wendel you cannot take everything someone tells you for face value. You are too educated and resourceful to be this ignorant about this topic."

At this moment in my life, academic journey, and in my ministry, I was also embarrassed at the ill-informed facts I had ingrained in my mind as truth. For years I had listened to media and stigmas as my source of information. I had allowed the views and perceptions of other people become my own. To my surprise, much of what I was exposed to were falsities. To think, here I was an educated, successful, Pastor and community leader who was still ignorant to HIV/AIDS. What I did realize in my moment of enlightenment was that I was only ignorant because of the fear I had within myself about this health issue. I had done like others and made it a moral matter. Researching and discovering the truths behind HIV/AIDS would have involved me tackling my own morality; but since HIV is also a virus that leads to death, I would also be faced to address my own mortality.

I believe there are many other Dead Christians who don't want to address HIV/AIDS because of their personal fears. Fears that include the thoughts, "People will think I have it", "People will think I'm gay", "People will think I'm promiscuous", "What if I get tested and I do have HIV?", "Will I die in a year?", "I can't imagine taking all those pills", and the worst thought of all...

"Sin is the root cause of HIV/AIDS"

If we are going to be Christians that are alive in the world we cannot be afraid of engaging with the issues that may make us feel uncomfortable. We cannot be afraid to dialogue with the leper as to how we can provide support, healing and restoration. In biblical accounts, it was leprosy that was the big health concern that caused others to be labeled as unclean. It was leprosy that placed people in a marginalized category. It was one of those incurable diseases that people stayed away from. Just like the lepers of Jesus' day, people living with HIV have been placed in a class and community by themselves. As a result we have limited their visibility and voice in our communities. We must be willing to offer the same platform of the breast cancer survivor to the person who is living with HIV/AIDS. We cannot continue to support the causes and illnesses that are trendy and ignore other illnesses that have become controversial. In the same way churches and ministries have "Pink Sundays" for breast cancer, we should also have "Red Sundays" to honor the courage of those in our community, and congregations, who are living with HIV/AIDS.

It is still alarming, with media and modern medical advancements, the number of people infected and affected by this health issue each year. "About 50,000 people get infected with HIV each year. In 2010, there were around 47,500 new HIV infections in the United States."[39] I believe these numbers will continue to rise as long as people remain irresponsible and ignorant about their personal health. I must restate for the Christian and religious community that HIV/AIDS is not a moral issue; as others have made it out to be. HIV/AIDS is a health issue. It does not matter how a person contracted the virus. As we have discovered, HIV is not only transmitted through sexual activity. With free testing now available, there is no excuse as to why people are still transmitting this virus to others unknowingly. The second we can break down the stigmas associated with HIV/AIDS, there will then be created a level of hope for those who are in ultimate need of healing.

Why has the church, and why have contemporary Christians, not taken the lead in providing healing, hope and help to people living with HIV? The answer is simple. In the same manner as the leper in biblical times, we have deemed those who have HIV/AIDS as unclean and untouchable. The first step to restoring the person is to acknowledge their personhood and not their condition. People living with HIV are people living with a medical condition. They are not dirty, or unworthy of our time and attention. We have also made the presupposition that people living with HIV acquired this health issue through some immoral action.

---

[39] Center for Disease Control and Prevention. 2015. *Basic Statistics*. September 14. www.cdc.gov/hiv/statistics/basics.html.

It has been a detriment to the advancement of healing for this community for people to assume that their illness is a result of something they have done. This reminds us of the same question that was often presented to Jesus in the biblical text, *"¹As Jesus was walking along, he saw a man who had been blind from birth. ²"Rabbi," his disciples asked him, "why was this man born blind? Was it because of his own sins or his parents' sins?" ³"It was not because of his sins or his parents' sins," Jesus answered. "This happened so the power of God could be seen in him." (John 9:1-3)* This assumption is another byproduct of social ignorance.

I personally know a woman who has HIV. She did not acquire it because she was same gender loving. She did not acquire it because she was promiscuous. She did not acquire it because she shared needles as a substance abuser. She acquired it through a blood transfusion while giving birth to her son. This happened a year before laws were put in place by the federal government to test blood for HIV before using it for medical purposes.

Is she immoral? Is she unclean? Does her testimony matter? Does she need support? When will modern Christians stop looking at the issues we are called to address, and see the people we are called to love through there life challenges?

I cannot close this section without allowing the numbers to speak for me. "About 1.2 million people in the United States were living with HIV at the end of 2012, the most recent year this information was available. Of those people, about 12.8% do not know they are infected."[40] I have echoed others with the statement, "The greatest risk associated with HIV is not knowing your status." It is known that a person becomes a greater threat to the health of others when they are unsure about their own health status. A person knowing their status is one of the primary ways I

---

[40] Center for Disease Control and Prevention. 2015. *Basic Statistics.* September 14. www.cdc.gov/hiv/statistics/basics.html.

believe we can combat this epidemic. With the advancement of modern technology, there are tests available to the general public that do not require a doctor's appointment or blood work. There are various at-home tests available at local drug stores. For those who may not be able to afford the common over-the-counter tests, there are various organizations that provide free testing. I believe the almost 13% that are unaware they are infected are too afraid of how traditional Christians and society will treat them once they discover their status.

It is a sad state of affair but a very true statement. Many people make the decision not to get tested in public forums because of the stigmas that have been associated with HIV. As an advocate for testing and education, and having hosted various free testing opportunities, I have seen first-hand how people will admit they have not been tested in over 6 months and have no desire to know their status! It baffles me at the number of people who remain selfish enough to place the health of others at risk because of their own insecurities and stigmas about this health issue.

Many people whom I have talked to living with HIV/AIDS have said one of their initial thoughts after being diagnosed was "how will people view me?" and "how will I be accepted by (insert community here)".

There are a number of Christians who have become so judgmental, not exclusively with HIV/AIDS but with other "morally connected" issues, that they look past the person who is desperate for compassion.

GLOBAL ILLITERACY

Global Illiteracy is so prevalent in our churches and traditional Christians don't even realize it. Often times I will visit churches and will see this social and academic issue being displayed right in our worship experiences. Every time I go to a church and there is some form of "community" reading I make it a point not to read. It's not because I don't want to read or because I'm being defiant. It's because there are occasions where I am curious as to the number of people who still struggle with reading. The first time I conducted this social experiment of personal observation in a church I was shocked! As I continued my unofficial studies it broke my heart. We cannot continue to assume that those who attend our worship experiences are all at the same academic level. While this is a very acceptable statement, my question for the current Christian is, "how will we help others excel academically?"

Whether it's a scripture, hymn, vision statement or mission statement being read in church, next time you are in a worship environment I challenge you to conduct the same experiment to see how many people in the audience have troubles reading.

Attempt to read the person's lips and you will quickly find out there are people we sit next to in church unable to read past a 5th grade reading level. "According to a study conducted in late April by the U.S. Department of Education and National Institute of Literacy, 32 million adults in the U.S. can't read. That's 14 percent of the population. 21 percent of adults in the U. S. read below a 5th grade level, and 19 percent of high school graduates can't read."[41] These numbers should prove shocking to you; a person who is actually reading! Your ability to comprehend, understand and retain information places you in a category where others struggle. Yet we will push that the reading of scripture is a religious practice that all Christians should participate in; whether public or private.

---

[41] Huffington Post. 2015. *The U. S. Illiteracy Rate Hasnt Changed in 10 Years.* October 2. www.huffingtonpost.com/2013/09/06/illiteracy-rate_n_3880355.html.

This, in my opinion, should not be viewed as some passive educational issue only to be handled by a broken educational system. To the same degree, provided this new information, it is almost impossible to trust the "household" to teach the next generation the importance of reading when the current generation of adults are illiterate. We wonder why the ignorance of humanity perpetuates? Because information is often transmitted through writing, then acquired through reading.

As a college professor of Biblical Heritage at Clark Atlanta University, I noticed this dynamic amongst my students as well. I will never forget my first semester teaching. As I would ask students to read certain literature and text, there were always a few students who struggled verbalizing the words that were printed before them. Global illiteracy is another issue I believe modern Christians need to champion. The problem with global illiteracy is that people who struggle with reading are embarrassed, and feel less then, when Rev. Dr. Pastor Deacon Michael Knowitall B.A., MBA, J.D. discovers they can't read. There is a reason why I started dropping many of my titles and intellectual accolades in certain environments. People should not feel intellectually inferior to another individual, especially a True Christian.

Because it doesn't matter how many books I've published if the audience I'm seeking to sell them to can't read them.

If the numbers I listed above don't make you angry or compassionate about global literacy you should turn in your "Christian Card". We cannot continue to preach being "students of the word" when a vast number of our congregations are illiterate. We cannot push for people to read and study the bible when a large majority are unable to get through Herman Melville's classic novel Moby Dick.

I am sure many people will blame the world's educational system. I am sure others will blame parenting. But I believe this is an area where True Christians should be stepping up to make sure those who struggle with reading can get tutoring and support. This is an area our Christian education departments should champion. Surprisingly, this isn't a social issue that costs a lot of money, time or resources to execute. All that is needed is a book and a willingness to serve. All that is needed is a few flash cards and a corner in a room. All that is needed is a dry erase board and a readiness to help. Sadly there are many contemporary Christians that bask in their intellect and obtain the mindset of, "well I have mine and you have yours to get". How can we push, and promote, vacation bible school and Sunday school when standard education has become a disparity? My recommendation does not involve an either/or approach in our churches but a both/and dynamic. While we are teaching the stories of David and Goliath, in addition to Jonah and the Whale, we should be ensuring our young believers have the opportunity to matriculate through the Psalms, Proverbs and the Gospels with ease.

Many people don't see a problem with this educational dilemma because it doesn't affect them directly. To my surprise, and I would hope to yours, actuality it does:

> "According to the Department of Justice, 'The link between academic failure and delinquency, violence, and crime is welded to reading failure.' The stats back up this claim: 85 percent of all juveniles who interface with the juvenile court system are functionally illiterate, and over 70 percent of inmates in America's prisons cannot read above a fourth grade level, according to BeginToRead.com."[42]

Are we beginning to see why this issue is important? Are we beginning to see the interconnectedness between academic latitude and social aptitude? Are we beginning to understand that to save the community should also involve preserving and advancing the mental and academic capacity? The correlation between reading

---

[42] Huffington Post. 2015. *The U. S. Illiteracy Rate Hasnt Changed in 10 Years.* October 2. www.huffingtonpost.com/2013/09/06/illiteracy-rate_n_3880355.html.

and delinquent behavior should push True Christians into action; if nothing for the purpose of making our communities safer. If we want to combat gang violence and community separation our efforts should be focused in the direction of supportive educational structures and initiatives.

Again, this is one of those issues that doesn't get much media attention or even social recognition. Yet it is an issue that effects almost every area of humanity. I would suggest those who can read to spend time teaching and exposing those who can't, or struggle with reading, to literature. Imagine the feeling of opening someone's consciousness to the amazing literature and information that circulates our world!

Outlined in this chapter were just a few areas I believe are crying for the attention of human agency. The above mentioned are areas of humanity that I am passionate about and am heavily involved in. I have seen first-hand how these disparities have crippled the world. I have observed these conditions of the marginalized. There are countless organizations and non-profits that have done the leg work and laid the foundation for service. I applaud these organizations for running the first leg of the race for those who are unable to run themselves. They have gathered the resources and are skilled in the fields they have been commissioned to serve. However my question becomes, how will True Christians help eradicate these problems? Will we make the conscious decision to join the race for human rights and privileges? Who will Christians begin to partner with in order to provide manpower and additional resources to these communities? How bad do these problems have to become before they warrant the attention of those who have been commissioned, by Jesus Himself, to carry out the solutions? I have heard elders say, "It will get worse before it gets better." I would like to re-coin this phrase to say…

It will get worse as long as Christians don't do better!

These are all moral, spiritual, humanitarian and ethical concerns. These issues only represent a small percentage of the work that needs to be done in our communities and around the globe. As Christians who preach a message of hope and live by the gospel of love, we should be the example of what the manifestation of hope and love looks like. As Dr. Lawrence E. Carter reminds us, "If we believe in our ethical values and principles, we commit ourselves and are loyal to causes that mirror our ethical viewpoints: if we believe that all people should have the same educational opportunities, we lobby the government to change laws."[43] However it is not just the educational objectives that we can lobby for. If we truly believe in the gospel message we preach on a weekly basis we should also desire to see that message take form in humanity. What we speak, and what we believe, should be evident in our actions towards society and humanity.

The issues of the world belong to us. The plights of others should become our causes. The work that has been left undone should be picked up by those who have the power, through God, to complete the task. We should be able to find our purpose in the passion of service. We should be willing to offer a hand up for those who have been perceived as desiring a hand out. For those who have lost their voices, we should sound the trumpet to notify them that help is on the way. As the army of Christ we cannot leave behind our wounded and forgotten soldiers. We are all in this thing called life together. As Paul encourages us in Galatians 6:2-3, "²Share each other's burdens, and in this way obey the law of Christ. ³If you think you are too important to help someone, you are only fooling yourself. You are not that important."

---

[43] Carter, Lawrence Edward, George David Miller, and Neelakanta Radhakrishnan. 2001. *Global Ethical Options*. Trumbull: Weatherhill.

EXPLAINING THE DECLINE IN CHURCH ATTENDANCE
What matters to the millennial?

The last thing a contemporary Christian wants to do is be around is other irrelevant Christians. For this reason many people make the conscious decision not to go to church. It's not that church environments are dead. There are great entertainment centers, we call churches, which people can go to! They have screens, lights, fog machines, young hip pastors in jeans, bright smiling greeters and, at The Worship Center, FREE COFFEE! So why are millennial Christians in the states still not attending church?

The truth is simple…all of the above mentioned doesn't matter the new millennial Christian.

Now don't get me wrong, the above mentioned enhancements to the contemporary worship experience are amazing. There was a moment in history when the church was dead and needed a revitalization for how we gathered for worship. To be honest, these advances have had a very positive influence on the 'worship' element of Christianity. The Dead Church heard the requests of the community and made the necessary adjustments in order to keep up with the times. However, the Christians of today are seeking more than just a Sunday morning worship experience. They are looking for a way to serve. They are looking for a way to get involved. They seek connections with their communities. They are looking for ways to give back. They are looking for a way to sincerely "connect back to God and humanity".

This text is not designed to help churches grow their membership. This book is not designed to help Pastors grow their ministry presence. I don't want people to feel as though I am bashing the church, or Christianity as a faith. I would understand if I was a non-religious person writing this text. But as an insider of the faith I am able to write from a very specific perspective. The purpose of this text is for all of us, who claim the Christian faith, to do a self-examination as to why we profess this faith. There are dozens of faith practices for a person to choose from. From Ancient Near Eastern, to Traditional Orthodox, African Derived and New Age, people have options. What I desire is to help those who have adopted the philosophies of this Traditional Orthodox religion to come home to the original brand, and message, of the faith. I believe there needs to be a call that refocuses our attention back to the message of Jesus. As with any philosophy or doctrine, time has taken its toll on the tenants of the faith. Since the inception of Christianity there have been various cultural, spiritual, and historical influences that have shaped and formed this religion.

In doing my own personal research, I was able to discover some very interesting opinions as to why Christians are no longer active in the church. Specifically the millennial or those who came into young adulthood around the year 2000. This community of people are those who have experienced an array of shifts in culture and economics. This generation has caused a change in society, job markets, technology, politics and economics to name a few. This generation has changed how we view education, service and the workforce. This group of people have also been able to shed new, and meaningful, light on religion and spirituality. I believe that their points of view can help us answer the following questions: Why are our corporate gatherings becoming depleted each week of attendees? Why are some of our mega churches turning into hallow arenas? Why are people taking the path of spirituality instead of religiosity? The funny thing is I was once a traditional Christian too. I guess you could say I had my "Paul on the road to Damascus encounter" one day. It was my point of personal discovery, and also came to be a point of personal purpose. However, instead of me going from Christian hater to Christian converter, I was a comfortable Christian who needed to be converted into an uncomfortable, or active, Christian.

Like many other millennial Christians, I have encountered both ends of the spectrum. At one point I was such a super Christian I had grown numb to the social issues outside of the church. In my childhood, and early youth, not going to church was not an option. I was involved in everything my time would allot for. On the other hand, there was a time when I was completely fed up with Christianity and had stop going to church for the reasons outlined in this book! You can call me crazy, but I have traveled down both roads. And I am grateful for the journey because it has lead me back to a place where I can bring healing and hope to the faith.

I remember the last time I "left the church" (because there was more than one occasion where I did). The level of hurt I felt as I drove off the parking lot that final time was immeasurable. As the tears began to well in my eyes I felt as though I could also fell the heart of God breaking for His people. I felt as though God was hurt regarding the condition of the church. I felt that God was experiencing a feeling of disappointment towards His creations. There was one instance that stands out in my memory; as I literally placed the church behind me and drove off the parking lot. It wasn't related to anything done to me, but I was hurt at how church people were treating non-church, and other churched, people. I was hurt at how Christians would turn their noses up and not want to sit next to the homeless gentleman in service. I was hurt at the gossip associated with the young lady who was discovered to be pregnant but not married. I was hurt at how some Christians were hurting other Christians. I was hurt at the number of "parking lot meetings" and after rehearsal stand arounds that only produced more drama and disconnection. I remember being in a church service and literally feeling the heart of God breaking for humanity.

> In my interview with Dr. William E. Flippin Sr., Pastor of The Greater Piney Grove Baptist Church in Atlanta, and Certified Life Coach, we discussed the findings of Pastor Gerald Brooks, Pastor of the Grace Outreach Center in Plano, TX that: Churches now compete with everything. Pastor Books notes that competition is anything which consumes people's time. Competition for the church is more intense than ever before. He makes the true statement in that Sunday isn't sacred anymore. Especially in the culture of the millennial, Sunday mornings aren't a priority. Social events, and secular functions, have moved from weekdays to Sundays. Even events that once made an attempt to honor the Sabbath have moved from Sunday afternoons to Sunday mornings. People view their commitment in terms which don't stack up to reality. He says that when we break down the actions, and commitments, of the modern millennial in church we will discover that 40% don't serve, 30% don't give and 25% attend another church. Brooks also points out that when people lose their equilibrium, God is the first thing to go. When times get hard, and the bearings of life begin to spiral downward, a person's connectivity to God is often the first to bite the bullet. It is easy to get out of balance with: caring for parents, children, jobs, life's challenges, feuds, family addition, marriage, death, cultural shifts. Instead of finding our root and bearings in God we search for other ways to take our focus off of stressful realities. He notes that the typical church member stays at a particular ministry, or church, 3.3 years.[44]

I believe the decline in church attendance, and involvement, is due to the fact that we have not connected our current missions to the assignment, and commission, of Christ. The reason I believe churches, and ministries, are experiencing a decline in attendance stems from the reason that they do not attend community events and initiatives. People are leaving the church because the church has left the community. If we are going to rebirth the church we are going to have to rebirth the church's

---

[44] Flippin, Dr. William E., interview by Dr. Wendel T. Dandridge. 2016. *Pastor of The Greater Piney Grove Baptist Church* (April 19).

involvement in the community. Need I remind you of the commission Jesus gave to the original seventy-two disciples?

> ¹The Lord now chose seventy-two other disciples and sent them ahead in pairs to all the towns and places he planned to visit. ²These were his instructions to them: "The harvest is great, but the workers are few. So pray to the Lord who is in charge of the harvest; ask him to send more workers into his fields. ³Now go, and remember that I am sending you out as lambs among wolves. (Luke 10:1-3)

Gene Wilkes also writes in *Jesus on Leadership* that filling organizational charts with warm bodies will certainly kill a church. Freeing God's people to serve as God has gifted them makes a church grow.[45] If the preceding makes a church grown then the counter will make a church decline. If we don't give people the opportunity to be free in their passions to serve we are only killing the Christian path to salvation. The longer we let talent and hunger sit in the seats of our pews, instead of allowing them to flourish in our communities, we are only staggering the faith.

We have the power to create the world we seek to manifest. However, this can only take place when we make the conscious decision to do what our hearts lead us to do. The world will become a better place when we all seek to be better people. What baffles me is the number of people who will sacrifice for the sake of society but not for the sake of humanity. As Nouwen suggests, People have lost naïve faith in the possibilities of technology and are painfully aware that the same powers that enable us to create new life styles also carry the potential for self-destruction.[46] If we are going to impact the nations we must be willing to put in the same effort for the spiritual as we do for the secular. The thought processes of the millennial is that what

---

[45] Wilkes, C. Gene. 1998. *Jesus on Leadership: Discovering the Secrets of Servant Leadership from the Life of Christ.* Wheaton: Tyndale House Publishers.

[46] Nouwen, Henri J. M. 1972. *The Wounded Healer: Ministry in Contemporary Society.* New York: Doubleday Religion.

we do for our nine to five jobs, we should be willing to do for God. As I share with those who work with The Worship Center Church, " if you can give a minimum of 160 hours to the CEO of your company per month, in return for wages, you can give one hour in service to humanity to God for the graces and mercy that are afforded to you daily."

HOW SUPER CHRISTIANS CAN BECOME DEAD CHRISTIANS

That's right, even the "Super Christian" can become a "Dead Christian"

At one point in my spiritual journey I had become very comfortable with my Christianity. I could have been the poster child for the "church boy" ad. At one point I was at the church 4 days a week. I attended 3-5 services a Sunday. I was in the music ministry, the Pastor of the young adult ministry, a Youth Pastor at one point, a children's church volunteer and much more! I preached. I sung. I directed the choir. I played the keyboard. I have done it all in the church. The problem was that everything I did served the churches I was a part of. I was caught in the cycle of church work. I wasn't serving humanity or the community half as much as I was serving the church. I wasn't volunteering with the local organizations and nonprofits half as much as I could have. I was so busy in church that I had no time to be in the community. I couldn't feed the homeless because I had choir rehearsal. I couldn't volunteer at the local Salvation Army because I had to be in staff meeting. I wasn't able to tutor or mentor a young student because I had to prepare the sermon I was scheduled to preach the following Sunday. I was engulfed in doing church work to the point where I had forgotten about my work for the kingdom. This was a problem.

However, and the end of the day I had to realize my Christianity had nothing to do with how many brownie points I got for going to church and doing church people stuff. What I did realize was that my Christian existence meant nothing if I wasn't following Jesus' ultimate commandment: to love and serve others. There was a time in my Christian journey where I had a serious conviction for my laziness in serving others. Here I was teaching, preaching and singing on Sunday morning, yet you would never see my face tending to the needs of the community. But then again I would notice other fellow Christians doing the same thing! Every time the church doors were opened they were front and center. Every time there was a convention or a conference they were the first to register. Every concert or musical would be packed with people looking to hear some great singing. However, when a call was put out to these same audiences for service the attendance would become fractional.

Church has become a place where love is a personality trait and not a character trait engrained in the molecular DNA of Christianity. People know we have love and the ability to love, but when will that love become real in the makeup of humanity? We know what love is. We run to the Corinthian scripture that helps us define this element of life:

> [1]If I could speak all the languages of earth and of angels, but didn't love others, I would only be a noisy gong or a clanging cymbal. [2]If I had the gift of prophecy, and if I understood all of God's secret plans and possessed all knowledge, and if I had such faith that I could move mountains, but didn't love others, I would be nothing. [3]If I gave everything I have to the poor and even sacrificed my body, I could boast about it; but if I didn't love others, I would have gained nothing.
> [4]Love is patient and kind. Love is not jealous or boastful or proud [5]or rude. It does not demand its own way. It is not irritable, and it keeps no record of being wronged. [6]It does not rejoice about injustice but rejoices whenever the truth wins out. [7]Love never gives up, never loses faith, is always hopeful, and endures through every circumstance.
> [8]Prophecy and speaking in unknown languages and special knowledge will become useless. But love will last forever! [9]Now our knowledge is partial and incomplete, and even the gift of prophecy reveals only part of the whole picture! [10]But when the time of perfection comes, these partial things will become useless.
> [11]When I was a child, I spoke and thought and reasoned as a child. But when I grew up, I put away childish things. [12]Now we see things imperfectly, like puzzling reflections in a mirror, but then we will see everything with perfect clarity. All that I know now is partial and incomplete, but then I will know everything completely, just as God now knows me completely.
> [13]Three things will last forever—faith, hope, and love—and the greatest of these is love. (1 Corinthians 13)

How does this text fit in the context of humanitarian service? The text lets us know that we can have all the education in the world and it mean nothing. We can be students of the academy for the purpose of intellectual advancement. But if we do not take that intellect to better the world we live in it becomes for not. A person can embody all of the spiritual gifts that serve the church. It is easy to identify a pastor, teacher, prophet and evangelist in our churches. However, where are the missionaries? Where are the ones who are taking their spiritual gifts to the world? We can have all the faith in healing and holiness. We can believe that God will deliver and showcase his ultimate power in the world. But can we take that same faith that God will work though us to be the extensions of love and hope in the community? We can give all we have empirically to display our humanitarian support. I know people who write big checks, and make large donations, for the purpose of showboating that they have the resources to give. But if we don't do it in the spirit of love it becomes a waste of energy and goods.

The text speaks of patience and kindness. Both of which are needed for the work, and service of Christ. We should administer acts of kindness on those who may not consistently receive love. To the same extent, we should be patient in the work that God does in order to bring others to restoration and reconciliation. The text speaks of us not being boastful or proud. We cannot take pride in what we do for God. We should adopt the spirit of humility in that what we do in the world is for God and his edification. We can't take pride in what God ultimately gives us the grace to do. Another piece of this text I admire is where it speaks on the fact that love does not rejoice in injustices but seeks truth for liberation. Love doesn't quit, and it doesn't lose the faith and hope in a better life.

The text lets us know that what we do, and accomplish, in life will fade away. Nothing is made to last forever. This truth applies to our lives in that, one day, this existence we call life on earth will be over. Generations down the line we, and what we've done, runs a great risk of being forgotten forever. It is only in our expressions of love that we leave a lasting impression. The word of God challenges us to mature in love as well. We should be aiming to grow, through love, to a level that makes us a mature Christian. We will remain infants in the faith as long as we don't nurture our desire to love others. We will continue to harbor bitterness, resentment, guilt and frustration with humanity as long as we operate in anything other than love. What is even more interesting in this text is that the author says that our faith and hope are important; however, love will always trump what we believe in and hope for.

We know how love is expressed. We are well aware of the types of love and forms of love that make their way into our lives. We know who we are called to love. We are commissioned to love the hopeless, the marginalized and the oppressed. We know where the love of Christ is needed most. It is needed on the corners of the world where communities of people have been forgotten. We understand the importance of Christ's love in the globe. For it was Jesus who, historically, gave us the ultimate example of doing for someone who cannot return the gesture to the same degree. So why don't we see love in action anymore? My hypothesis is that the heartbeat of God is faint in the workings of humanity. Dead Christians are to blame, but dead churches have birth these zombies.

If you are wondering why Christians, in the United States, no longer attend church, I may have the answer. I believe, with the help of a few scholars and commentators, I have discovered a few very valid arguments to this topic and observation of the American church. There may be a few of the below listed opinions that you, as a Christian, dead or "alive", can relate to.

Again, the purpose of this text is informational and thought provoking. However, I hope we can all take a moment to reflect and to ask ourselves the serious question, "why am I a Christian?". But more importantly, "What am I doing in order to help make humanity better as a Christian?". Our Christian lifestyle has to be more than just about the communal worship experience. It must go beyond the 10am hour on Sunday mornings and the 7pm hour on Wednesday nights. Worship, prayer and devotion should not be the only practices that feed us spiritually. We cannot be satisfied, on our quest to heaven, if we do not create the kingdom of God here on earth. I believe this desire for more service in the Christian experience is what has caused many people to leave the church; and ultimately organized religion.

I am of the belief people stopped asking the hard questions of the church and decided to do a little self-examination. What they discovered was that the only person to blame was themselves. I believe what they discovered was that the church was not at fault; rather it was the people in the church who held the responsibility. I believe people stopped making the excuse of the organized church not doing enough. Instead the excuse was connected to personal will and desire.

As stated earlier, there are a plethora of reasons people make the conscious decision not to attend church. I agree with one writer, in their opinion, as to one of the primary reasons people don't attend church. This person states it is because:

> "There is no reason to. You've made it too easy...We want something more ancient than sign on the dotted line. But if membership means an invitation to study the mystery of faith deeply, to put some skin in the game with time and talent and treasure, to enter into a process of formation over the next few months whereby we openly discuss the tenants of faith."[47]

The modern millennial doesn't just want to go to church; they want to be an expression of the church in humanity. I believe there should be a church overhaul as to how we acclimate people through Christianity. Discipleship is a process and I believe we have strayed from effective methods that create honorable disciples. I believe the church has mastered bringing people "to" Christ. The church must be

---

[47] Unknown. 2015. *Here are 3 reasons no one is joining your church (plus one more)*. October 13. www.reluctantxian.wordpress.com/2015/10/13/here-are-3-reasons-no-one-is-joining-your-church-plus-one-more.

applauded for its ability to get people through the doors. A heart breaking observation is that those doors are also revolving. People come into our churches and leave back out because they have not made a connection with the message of Christ. If people truly joined themselves to the words of Jesus they would never leave the community in service. I believe the downfall is that the church fails in the area of walking people "through" Christianity. We don't take the time to truly develop and train new, or returning, Christians.

It is simple to find a church, be moved by the worship experience, accept Christ, and gain membership. But what happens after this moment of emotional and spiritual response? If we chose to adopt the book of Acts model, every person who came would then be prompted to serve and connect. I must restate that I am not talking about all churches in America. There are ministries that have systems in place to ensure that people are connected to the mission of Christ. Their passion for service is passed on to those who God has sent their way. Unfortunately there are not many ministries who push service and connection; nevertheless much of what is presented as opportunities are self-serving for the church.

You may be encouraged to join the choir. You could be recruited as a Children's Church volunteer. You may be asked to serve on the guest services team or to join a gender specific group. My question is how many ministries have an outline of community projects for people to Jump!n to and serve? Often time's people are prompted and cheered to join a ministry within the church. I believe the true problem falls with the fact that many churches don't have much happening outside the church for people to be involved in. Imagine the impact our churches would have if we began asking the question, "Where would you like to serve outside our church?".

THE MESSAGE TO BECOME A FOLLOWER OF CHRIST

My primary inquiry in this text pushes the question, as it relates to how many Christians will chose to become true "followers" of Christ?

What do you think of when you hear the word 'follower'? What comes to mind when you heard the phrase 'follower of Christ'? When I hear this term I jump to the conclusion that in order for a person to be determined as a "follower" of Christ it would mean that this individual is going somewhere. The word follow is considered to be a verb or action word. Should we continue to dissect this phrase, "Christ" is the title given to Jesus because of his message of service and social justice. Therefore, if we are going to be "Followers of Christ" we have to be moving in the direction of Jesus' message to serve and create social change. It is as simple as that. The church has to leave the building. There is no way possible that a person can be labeled as a follower if they are choosing to stay in the same position. This does not solely translate as a physical location, but also a state of mind, moral obligation and character. Christians should be constantly responding to the message and example of Christ.

We should be consistently moving in the direction of Christ's actions and not just Christ's words. True Christians are going places in the world. I believe people are drawn to Christianity for a reason. There is a reason that people are attracted to the faith of Christianity. It is our responsibility, as True Christian, to keep this magnetic draw strong by putting our energy out in humanity. We should be the connection point that allows people to bridge the gap between their humanness and their spiritual self. There should be such an energy that permeates the service of Christians that it not only pushes the message of Jesus, but also prompts people to move with the message. Our actions should motivate and encourage others to get involved in the work of Christ. People should see Christians making a difference and feel compelled to join the movement to end the countless global disparities that are out in our communities.

The foundation of Christianity was based on the practice of discipleship. It was centered on the concept of creating likeminded, or like consciousness, individuals. The basis of the faith encompassed the notion that we could teach others to be more Christ like. In our efforts to make disciples of men we should keep in mind the charge the original disciples were given. Before we fast forward into the modern church, I believe we should take a stroll to the edges of the water in the biblical city of Jerusalem. Here we find the first disciples being called to the service of discipleship. Before we can enter the building we have named the church, I believe we should visit the church without walls. There are three accounts in the scriptures that have one common thread that I believe we can gleam from in today's consciousness.

> [18]One day as Jesus was walking along the shore of the Sea of Galilee, he saw two brothers—Simon, also called Peter, and Andrew—throwing a net into the water, for they fished for a living. [19]Jesus called out to them, "Come, follow me, and I will show you how to fish for people!" [20]And they left their nets at once and followed him. (Matthew 4:18-20)

> [1]One day as Jesus was preaching on the shore of the Sea of Galilee, great crowds pressed in on him to listen to the word of God. [2]He noticed two empty boats at the water's edge, for the fishermen had left them and were washing their nets. [3]Stepping into one of the boats, Jesus asked Simon, its owner, to push it out into the water. So he sat in the boat and taught the crowds from there. [4]When he had finished speaking, he said to Simon, "Now go out where it is deeper, and let down your nets to catch some fish." [5]"Master," Simon replied, "we worked hard all last night and didn't catch a thing. But if you say so, I'll let the nets down again." [6]And this time their nets were so full of fish they began to tear! [7]A shout for help brought their partners in the other boat, and soon both boats were filled with fish and on the verge of sinking. [8]When Simon Peter realized what had happened, he fell to his knees before Jesus and said, "Oh, Lord, please leave me—I'm too much of a sinner to be around you." [9]For he was awestruck by the number of fish they had caught, as were the others with him. [10]His partners, James and John, the sons of Zebedee, were also amazed. Jesus replied to Simon, "Don't be afraid! From now on you'll be fishing for people!" [11]And as soon as they landed, they left everything and followed Jesus. (Luke 5:1-11)

[16]One day as Jesus was walking along the shore of the Sea of Galilee, he saw Simon and his brother Andrew throwing a net into the water, for they fished for a living. [17]Jesus called out to them, "Come, follow me, and I will show you how to fish for people!" [18]And they left their nets at once and followed him. [19]A little farther up the shore Jesus saw Zebedee's sons, James and John, in a boat repairing their nets. [20]He called them at once, and they also followed him, leaving their father, Zebedee, in the boat with the hired men. (Mark 1:16-20)

There are a few common threads between these accounts of the first disciples: obedience and a willingness to forgo the familiar to embark on a journey towards Christ consciousness. The first thing we must learn to do, as students and disciples of the word, is to be obedient to the permissive will and way of our heavenly father. If we are unwilling to be obedient, then the commission will become a thought of moral consciousness and not a method for action. We must be willing to obey this commandment that Jesus puts out in His New Testament message and account. When we analyze the text we find that Jesus discovers his first disciples in a place where they were familiar. Jesus finds most of his first disciples already working in their vocation and passion. What are the things you are passionate about that will lead you closer to God? I am a firm believer in that the moment we choose to give the gifts God has bestowed upon us back to God is the moment we find our purpose.

So why are Christians not embracing this model of service or learning to follow the root of Christ's ministry? Why has service, social justice and community involvement not been engrained in the mindset of all Christians after they walk down the aisle of the church? Why has the current generation of Christians not been introduced to the importance of missionary work? The fact of the matter is that contemporary Christians are tired of being lazy! The current generations of people who want to be a part of organized religion need a sense of belonging. True Christians should be tired of the only qualification for membership (into the faith) being tithing and church attendance.

I believe one of the primary issues associated with the reason people have strayed from the essence of the faith is the lack of discipleship. Teaching others how to serve has been one of the major downfalls of the church. To the same degree, non-active Christians are only breeding other non-active Christians. In our churches, small groups and personal conversations are we teaching service? When we gather are we gathering for the purpose of social advancement and planning? Are we creating the dialogue between seasoned Christians and new Christians as to the importance of humanitarian action? Are we sharing our stories on how service influenced our own lives? What I have noticed is that much of what is taught is a self-serving theology.

I blame Pastors and other religious leaders for creating this consciousness of me, myself, and I in the context of the church. Some of the only times we engage in service dialogue is during the holiday season when we are made aware of the poverties around us. It is not until commercials cross our television screens that remind us that there are others in the world who do not experience the same graces we share. It is not until we see the person with the bell in front of the mall asking us to place our change in the red tin bucket that we are reminded of the disparities of others. The world would be a better place if we had continuous conversation about our Christian obligations.

You, should you be a person who professes the Christian faith, should be desiring more from your faith. Not from the church, but from your life; from your personal connection with the Divine. You should be challenging your churches, and your Pastors, to challenge you more. If we want to see the church change we have to demand it. If we want to see the church change we have to quit excepting the norm. If we want to see a change in the church we have to require more of ourselves. At The Worship Center, I believe the reason people have been joining our ministry is because I, as their Pastor, refuse to just let people except Christ and do nothing for humanity. There has to be a sense of responsibility and accountability.

Most Christians know they should be serving. Most Christians know they should be giving. Most Christians have the feeling that Christianity is more than what they are presently experiencing. Most Christians know they should be raising the moral standards of life and community. Yet many traditional Christians feel no push towards service. However, what all Christians should understand is that when we meet the divine we will have to give an account for what we did while we experienced this consciousness called life. God isn't going to exclusively ask you how many times you prayed and went to church. God may, however, ask you how many times you visited the sick. You may be asked what you did to end the spread of HIV in underserved communities. You may be asked how you improved the literacy of children in countries where education is limited. God will say, "I gave you the gift of eternal life, what did you do to help others live?"

The church should be an exciting place for people to jump in and get involved. It should be a place where an individual knows they can connect to the heartbeat of God in the community. It should be a place where we are open about our abilities and resources to do for others. Do you feel as though *"Your church is depressed?"*[48] This is another reason why many contemporary Christians, including yourself, may not attend church. According to this writer, to look at the modern church can be analogues to watching a sad movie. To view the church today can cause a person to lose hope in the message and original model of Christ. Outside of the lights and fog machines on Sunday morning, there is nothing compelling and exciting about formalized church that pushes Christians to connect with humanity. The truth is there are countless people who leave church, after every gathering experience, with no sense of service. It is becoming more evident that there are countless frustrated

---

[48] Unknown. 2015. *Here are 3 reasons no one is joining your church (plus one more).* October 13.
www.reluctantxian.wordpress.com/2015/10/13/here-are-3-reasons-no-one-is-joining-your-church-plus-one-more.

Christians who have become fed up with the emotionalism of ministry and are now seeking opportunities to serve.

The Pastor may have great oratorical skills. The Children's ministry may cater to newborns and advance with service through college ages. Small groups and house meetings have become very popular in the modern church. The seating in the auditorium may be comfortable. Professional, and skilled, singers and musicians now lead our worship. But the millennials of today want to get excited about what they are able to bring to the table. The millennials of today, as narcissistic as it may be, are eager to take a selfie of themselves giving a plate of food to a homeless person. There are tons of great churches that offer a depressing service agenda. Yet we wonder why seats in our sanctuaries are empty.

We cannot continue to profess the faith of Christianity if we are unwilling to do the work of Christ. It is not an either or situation, but rather it is a both-and willingness. We must learn to find the balance between the two. What I have observed is that there is no balance or blend amongst the millennial believer. In my environment I have observed that there are two types of Christians: The Church goers and the community servers. What is even more interesting is how these two audiences of people very rarely meet. Those who are committed to church functions rarely come out to support community functions. On the other hand there are other communities of disciples who don't place Sunday worship as a top priority, but will be the first ones to respond when there is a project that needs to be done in the community. To dwell on one end of these spectrums, I believe, creates an unhealthy spiritual diet. Both, as the bible encourages us in the book of Ecclesiastes, are important as we grow closer to Christ.

> [1]*For everything there is a season, a time for every activity under heaven. [2]A time to be born and a time to die. A time to plant and a time to harvest. [3]A time to kill and a time to heal. A time to tear down and a time to build up. [4]A time to cry and a time to laugh. A time to grieve and a time to dance. [5]A time to scatter stones and a time to gather stones. A time to embrace and a time to turn away.*

> *⁶A time to search and a time to quit searching. A time to keep and a time to throw away. ⁷A time to tear and a time to mend. A time to be quiet and a time to speak. ⁸A time to love and a time to hate. A time for war and a time for peace. (Ecclesiastes 3:1-8)*

If we are going to progress the faith we are going to have to learn how to create a healthy balance. One is not more important than the other. No group will have special seating in heaven over the other. Neither group is better, or 'more Christian', than the other. Both points of view and both decisions of Christian practice have their perspective place. We have to see the importance of feeding our spirit person (through worship) along with our humanitarian nature (through service). We must first understand ourselves as spiritual beings having a human experience. Miguel writes in his book that, "The false dichotomy existing between faith (love the Lord your God) and ethics (love your neighbor as yourself) is collapsed by Jesus, who demands manifestations of both by those wishing to be called his disciples. The doing of love becomes the new commandment Christians are called to observe."[49] At its root we should understand that love is an action word. What we can also conclude is that to be a disciple is to act in the community as well. Jesus lets us know through His example that we need both the love for God and the love for one another to be counted among other true disciples. We cannot continue to be Christians who adopt a partial theology of the message of Jesus Christ. Either we will embrace the entire message or remain unproductive as disciples.

Aristotle says, "For the things we have to learn before we can do them, we learn by doing them, e.g. men become builders by building and lyreplayers by playing the lyre; so too we become just by doing just acts, temperate by doing temperate acts, brave by doing brave acts."[50] In my opinion we become disciples by doing what

---

[49] Torre, Miguel A De La. 2004. *Doing Christian Ethics from the Margins.* Maryknoll: Orbis Books.

[50] Aristotle. 1997. *Nichomachean Ethics.* London: Wordsworth.

disciples do. We become more loving by expressing love. We manifest peace when we show ourselves as peaceful. We become agents of change when we chose to be the change we seek. We have the potential to manifest a greater community when we make the conscious effort to do community work. What Aristotle is pushing us towards is a pragmatic and practical theology. What we are challenged towards in today's generation is the importance of manifesting a living gospel; making the word of God real in the world. More importantly we should be making the word of God relevant for today's listener and practitioner.

It requires a certain level of courage to be a true disciple in today's world. With religion as a central focal point in the media, one must be aware that to make this stand may bring more attention to the faith. The moment we begin giving attention to those who have been intentionally placed in the shadows is also the moment the spotlight will be placed on the faith. What we find in the biblical text is that Jesus' attention to the marginalized, and the oppressed, caused a ruckus in the community. His actions make a very strong, and bold, statement to the religious leaders of his time. What it did in the long haul of things would cause other religious leaders to fear the hard, and meaningful, word for God. What we can learn from Jesus is that, as Wilkes states, leaders make bold decisions. Those who follow are either amazed or afraid.[51] Jesus pulls both of these emotions out of the leaders of His day. To the same extent we should also feel a tug on our hearts to make bold decisions that impact our community today.

We cannot become so grand and comfortable that we forget our commission to serve others with the love of Christ. Wilkes points out a conversation said between Jesus, John and James as a prime example for how we cannot forget our Christian essence amid our personal positions. Jesus answered James and John with the

---

[51] Wilkes, C. Gene. 1998. *Jesus on Leadership: Discovering the Secrets of Servant Leadership from the Life of Christ.* Wheaton: Tyndale House Publishers.

response, "What do you want me to do for you?" (Mark 10:36) In this one statement Jesus turns the pyramid of authority upside down. He reminds us, in this one statement, that even the greatest amongst us should still showcase a heart for service. I am sure that James and John never would have imagined that the Son of God would inquire what He could do for them. However what Jesus shows us as a result of his statement is that servant leaders accept the honest requests of those they serve.[52] Jesus shows us that servant leaders should have their ears to the voices of those who we have been called to serve.

In this text Jesus demonstrates that there is no separation between the leader and the followers. Jesus also becomes the example for those who profess that they have been called into religious leadership. If we are bold enough to make the statement that we have been called to lead Christians into a closer relationship with Christ, we should also be bold enough to stand in the gap for those who have been ostracized in our communities. Instead of asking for more from our congregations, we should be asking our communities what our congregations can do for them. This not only bridges a gap, but it also opens up a safe space for community dialogue.

What we can learn from the lessons, and model, of Jesus is that the root of community and discipleship are all encompassed in the heart of relationship building. What we find throughout the biblical text is a Jesus who spends time with his disciples. What we find in the biblical text is a Jesus who is open to listening to the needs of his followers. What we find in the text is a Jesus who sits on the hillsides of Jerusalem and engages in conversation with the crowds. If we are going to be Christians who are agents of change we must first be willing to be people unafraid of building relationships. James Burns writes that relationship is everything in leadership. Burns notes that leadership is relational. Leaders lead most effectively when relationships

---

[52] Wilkes, C. Gene. 1998. *Jesus on Leadership: Discovering the Secrets of Servant Leadership from the Life of Christ*. Wheaton: Tyndale House Publishers.

are open and strong between them and their followers.[53] This is the primary reason Jesus became so well known in his community. The connections he made with others challenged his environment to tear down the walls of separation that disconnected the church from the community; religious persons from the common individual. If we are going to remain effective we must be willing to stand in front of the woman caught in adultery. If we are to remain relevant we must be willing to accept the tax collector and the fisherman as our friends and co-laborers in ministry.

The earnest desire to spread the message of Christ is not enough. If we are going to transform the world we live in we must have the willingness to do different and to be different. We must have the willingness to engage where others have let go. We must be willing to accept those who have been socially rejected by others. We must be willing to go in the trap houses and the houses of the single parent living with government assistance. We must be willing to take health services to the homeless populations of our area. We must be willing to hold the hand of the individual living with HIV as a partner to end this health epidemic. As Gene Wilkes writes, ambition is not the same thing as willingness to follow Jesus to the cross.[54] We have to be willing to suffer as Christ suffered. We must be willing to suffer in the same way the early disciples and apostles did. Philippians 1:27-29 tells us:

> *"27 Above all, you must live as citizens of heaven, conducting yourselves in a manner worthy of the Good News about Christ. Then, whether I come and see you again or only hear about you, I will know that you are standing together with one spirit and one purpose, fighting together for the faith, which is the Good News. 28 Don't be intimidated in any way by your enemies. This will be a sign to them that they are going to be destroyed, but that you are going to be saved, even by God himself. 29 For you have been given not only the privilege of trusting in Christ but also the privilege of suffering for him. 30 We are in this struggle together. You have seen my struggle in the past, and you know that I am still in the midst of it."*

---

[53] Burns, James MacGregor. 1978. *Leadership.* New York: Harper & Row.

[54] Wilkes, C. Gene. 1998. *Jesus on Leadership: Discovering the Secrets of Servant Leadership from the Life of Christ.* Wheaton: Tyndale House Publishers.

Jesus talks about suffering throughout his ministry on earth. On various occasions Jesus eludes to this notion that be a Christ follower would involve some uncomfortable moments. Jesus foreshadows the fact that the road of discipleship is not an easy one. Jesus mentions that a person should consider the cost before they accept the call. Jesus asked James and John a question that exposed their ambitious hearts and misconceptions about kingdom leadership in the New Testament. Jesus couched his question in the language of that day. He asked, "Can you drink the cup I drink or be baptized with the baptism I am baptized with?" (Mark 10:38) If we were to analyze this text in its context we can conclude that Jesus was referring to his suffering and death by this question. Jesus was essentially asking, "Are you willing to go through what I am prepared to go through for the liberation of humanity from sin?" The cup was an Old Testament symbol for suffering. Jesus used this same image of suffering in the Garden of Gethsemane on the night he was betrayed. He asked his Father in heaven, "Take this cup [of suffering on the cross] from me. Yet not what I will, but what you will" (Mark 14:36) If Jesus suffered with suffering then so will we. But in the same way that Jesus prayed for the will of his Father so should we.

There is so much we can learn from the example of Jesus. There is so much that we can learn from Jesus' teachings and parables. There is a lot that we can learn from Jesus' interactions with the community. There is much we can gleam from Jesus' interactions with the oppressed and the marginalized. One thing I will later discuss in this text is how we can become better Christians by adopting Christ's consciousness about the environment around him. Wilkes reminds us that following is at the core of being a servant leader. The word disciple means "learner."[55] If Jesus gave us the example, we should be open to adopting it as our personal model for Christian living. While churches, and Pastors, encourage us to be students of the word I also believe that we should be pupils of the life of Jesus and the early disciples.

---

[55] Wilkes, C. Gene. 1998. *Jesus on Leadership: Discovering the Secrets of Servant Leadership from the Life of Christ.* Wheaton: Tyndale House Publishers.

The decision to follow Jesus, and to lead the people of God, involves a tradeoff. When we look at the biblical model of discipleship Wilkes also points out that Jesus called his disciples to follow him first. In return they became leaders only after Jesus empowered them to lead. The question then becomes how did he empower them? The text demonstrates that He empowered them by insisting they follow him first.[56] In Matthew 16:24-28 we see the bridge of suffering, empowerment and discipleship coming together:

> *"24 Then Jesus said to his disciples, 'If any of you wants to be my follower, you must turn from your selfish ways, take up your cross, and follow me. 25 If you try to hang on to your life, you will lose it. But if you give up your life for my sake, you will save it. 26 And what do you benefit if you gain the whole world but lose your soul? Is anything worth more than your soul? For the Son of Man will come with his angels in the glory of his Father and will judge all people according to their deeds. 28 And I tell you the truth, some standing here right now will not die before they see the Son of Man coming in his Kingdom."*

Wilkes states that Jesus teaches that we learn to lead by learning to follow.[57] There are a few points of departure that we can take from this text in particular:

> 1. If we are going to be true disciples we have to put aside our own selfish intents. We must adopt the mindset that it is not about us. We must have the consciousness that there are others in the world who are in need of the grace of God also. We cannot continue to do things for our own benefit. Rather we should seek to make our actions to profit others.

> 2. If we are going to be true disciples we must be willing to share the burden of the cross in our communities. No one church can do it alone. No one denomination can do it alone. No religious organization can do it by themselves. We have to be open to sharing the load. We all have to bring our resources together to pitch in for the solution of a better world.

---

[56] Wilkes, C. Gene. 1998. *Jesus on Leadership: Discovering the Secrets of Servant Leadership from the Life of Christ.* Wheaton: Tyndale House Publishers.

[57] Wilkes, C. Gene. 1998. *Jesus on Leadership: Discovering the Secrets of Servant Leadership from the Life of Christ.* Wheaton: Tyndale House Publishers.

3. If we are going to be true disciples we must be willing to let go of the comfortabilities of our own lives for the sake of others. In American society most persons live a very comfortable life in comparison to others around the globe. As disciples we must be willing to forgo our graces in order to extend grace to others.

4. If we are going to be true disciples we should embrace the understanding that to gain here on earth is of least importance. We must be reminded that our heavenly rewards will be given based on our deeds here on earth, not our possessions.

Are we hearing for the voice of God in an effort to be obedient to His desire in our lives? Are we allowing his word to take root in the essence of our soul? The final expect of discipleship involves our obedience to actually do the above mentioned. According to Henri Nouwen, a root concept for the verb obey in the two biblical languages and Latin is "to listen"[58] I would suggest that our display of obedience has a direct connection to our ability to listen. What we do for God should have a direct connection to what we hear from God. In Luke 11:28 Jesus echoes this idea when he says, "Blessed rather are those who hear the word of God and obey it." These two traits are inseparable. Yet, for many modern Christians they hear the cries of help in humanity, yet still choose not to be a part of the healing process. There are numerous scriptures where Jesus challenges us to obedience. One account is found in the book of John the 14th chapter:

> *"23Jesus replied, 'All who love me will do what I say. My Father will love them, and we will come and make our home with each of them. 24 Anyone who doesn't love me will not obey me. And remember, my words are not my own. What I am telling you is from the Father who sent me. 25 I am telling you these things now while I am still with you. 26 But when the Father sends the Advocate as my representative-that is, the Holy Spirit- he will teach you everything and will remind you of everything I have told you." John 14:23-26*

---

[58] McNeill, Donald P, Douglas A Morrison, and Henri J. M. Nouwen. 1983. *Compassion: A Reflection on the Christian Life.* New York: Doubleday.

Henri Nouwen and his coauthors observed this about Jesus' life: Obedience, as it is embodied in Jesus Christ, is a total listening, a giving attention with no hesitation or limitation, a being "all ear"…When used by Jesus, the word obedience has no association with fear, but rather is the expression of his most intimate, loving relationship. Jesus' actions and words are the obedient response to this love of his Father.[59] Obedience is simply translating what you hear into action. But it is not just about action. It is about correct action. It is about an action that forces change. It is about an action that awakens the moral conscious of others. It is an action that challenges the status quo. It is an action that makes the norm abnormal. It is an action that makes people want to be better people. The disciples of today are synonymous with agents of change.

---

[59] McNeill, Donald P, Douglas A Morrison, and Henri J. M. Nouwen. 1983. *Compassion: A Reflection on the Christian Life.* New York: Doubleday.

THE ENTERTAINMENT OF MINISTRY AS A SMOKE SCREEN TO SERVICE

Please don't confuse entertainment with excitement?

Have we allowed our perfection in worship become a cover up for our lack of service in our local, and global communities? Have we become so great at doing Sunday morning worship that we overlook the needs of our communities on Friday nights? I am a firm believer that the worship experience should be more than just a Sunday morning show. I also believe that the Sunday morning experience should overflow into the remainder of the week through our service. What we experience and learn on Sunday should also be displayed in our everyday walk and encounters. I believe that people should be getting excited about the Christian work and involvement that happens outside of the four walls of the sanctuary. When will Christians come to a place where we challenge ourselves to be genuinely excited about service and being a part of global change as we are about communal worship?

Maybe contemporary Christians have nothing to get excited about. There is a population of American Christians who could care less about what their church does in, and for, the community. Their mentality is conditioned by their belief that "as long as I go to church" I am an ok Christian. Maybe Christianity has become a religion that "sub-surfaces" everything else. Can you remember a time when Christians prided themselves as being the best in social, community and humanitarian efforts? Do you recall a time in history where the church, and Christian model, was the go-to example for how moral obligation was executed in the world? I remember when people got excited about community block parties and vacation bible school. I remember when the church opened their doors to all, and all showed up to participate. Now, people have separated themselves so far from the church experience. Now, people will walk by a church with no concern, or consciousness, that it is even there. Part of the reason, I believe, is because we've perfected the worship experience at the expense of community outreach. Now "You do nothing well. We live in a time where excellence is highly desired."[60] We live in a day and age where the millennial believer desires a well-rounded spiritual community to associate with. A community of believers who strive for excellence in all things; worship and community work. Many Christians and churches can't take pride for anything that actually has substance to it!

It is disheartening the few that are carrying the message of service and moral obligation are doing it in their own name and not the name of Christ. It pains my heart to see the number of people who say they are servants to the community when in reality they have their own hidden agendas. It also pains my heart to see people who have abused the system of benevolence and have made businesses out of the donations given by others. Churches have ministry after ministry for every cause known to man: women's ministry, youth and young adult ministry, ushers ministry, pastor's aide ministry, praise and worship ministry, and the list goes on. Yet, very little of what they do is at a level where it makes an impactful difference in the community. The majority of the above mentioned ministries meet and have church functions, but very few of them will gather to support a community event.

Can we, for the sake of conversation, admit that true excellence is far from the mindset of some millennial Christians? That the quest to be the best at anything spiritual is far outside of our mental reach. We have no problem striving to be the best in our academics. We don't see a problem with being the best in our relationships. We typically find the millennial striving for excellence in their career or professional field. So why can't we do the same in our Christian walk and spiritual journey? To the same capacity, our desire to be the moral example for all things right and honorable isn't close to the level it needs to be. Right and moral living isn't always on the

---

[60] Unknown. 2015. *Here are 3 reasons no one is joining your church (plus one more).* October 13. www.reluctantxian.wordpress.com/2015/10/13/here-are-3-reasons-no-one-is-joining-your-church-plus-one-more.

forefront of our consciousness. To the same extent we don't find this thought process consistently taught in our churches. We still find churches, and religious leaders, who preach a self-serving theology and not a message of personal responsibility in humanity. And we wonder why millennial Christians refuse to keep attending none relevant churches.

Let's be honest, as I discussed in the previous chapter, your ability to even read this book places you at an intellectual level far greater than the level of millions in our world. The grace that God has blessed you with should not be seen by others but also experienced by others. With the advances in technology, information can literally travel at the speed of one click. There is no excuse that we cannot share the love of Christ with others. On the other hand what technology has done, in consequence, is raised the level of expectation of 'ministry' amongst millennial Christians. No longer can a religious leader tell their parishioners what to do without receiving a who, when, where or why response. No longer can the excuse "we don't have the resources' be used to explain why things can't be done in the community. We must remember there was a time in history where the church was the place to receive information. We have to recall that there were days were people went to the church as a model for breaking the barriers and norms of its day.

In history, certain cultures depended on the religious leader to educate them about certain elements of life. The religious leader was considered the wise one. When education was scarce, one of the most revered positions was that of the Pastor. In present day, there are people that attend church with neuroscience engineering degrees. Yet Pastors, and religious leaders, still believe that a 'call' from God is what will earn them the respect of the community. My challenge to the contemporary church leader is to push their followers to a place there they chose to break the norms of today. This is what will earn respect in our communities.

Returning to the observation of the contemporary American church, we should remain conscious of our intents and actions as we press towards the expansion of the faith. We cannot stray from the original message of Christ to the extent to where we no longer appear Christian. We cannot get so caught up in doing church that we forget to do the work or Christ. We cannot be so focused on bible studies if we are unwilling to be obedient to the word of God. If we are going to place the tag of "church" or "ministry" at the end of our organization titles we must be cautious to stay true to the essence of those identities. Aristotle says that we must examine the nature of actions, namely how we ought to do them; for these determine also the nature of the states of character that are produced.[61] I agree with Aristotle in that we should place our actions juxtapose to the intentions of our heart. We should be consistently asking ourselves the question, does this deed run parallel to message of the gospel. We should also be placing our ethical intentions (our ought) with the conscience of Christ. The fact of the matter is that we 'should' do what Christ encourages us to do because it comes from a consciousness of what 'ought' to be done in the world.

Service to humanity comes from a place of what is right and what is noble in the eyes of God and man. I agree with Aristotle in that when we do this process of evaluation we are able to protect the character, or essence, in which we operate in those things. When people see that Christians are acting as Christian for the sake of humanity's advancement, the brand, as I will discuss later in this text, will gain greater credibility amongst the other brands of faith. The character of Christianity is in question amongst many millennial believers. We can protect the faith the moment we make the conscious decisions to be the example of humanitarian service.

---

[61] Aristotle. 1997. *Nichomachean Ethics.* London: Wordsworth.

We wonder why our evangelistic efforts to reach the lost are ineffective. I believe the reason stems from our inability to create a culture where people feel connected to the heart of service and the original message of Christ. The number of converts that appear in the early church can manifest themselves in today's churches if we preach a gospel of humanitarian love and social responsibility. We cannot continue to preach a water downed, general love for people and a Christian responsibility to self-service. Mary Boys gives us an interesting idea of evangelism defined and subdivided. She says that, "Perhaps a broad, working definition will best reveal the full range of evangelism: preaching or teaching the scriptures in such a way as to arouse conversion.[62] We have to return to the basics of Christ's message for the world. We should revisit the text with a new lens of consideration. We should be mindful that our interpretation of this age old document will determine its vitality for future generations to come. Has the gospel become stale? Has the biblical text lost its fire? And is it because the proclaimers of this gospel have lost their zeal and connectivity with its message?

---

[62] Boys, Mary C. 1989. *Educating in Faith.* Lima: Academic Renewal Press.

HOW MODERN MILLENNIALS AND INTELLECTUALS VIEW THE CHURCH

Can we face the fact that modern millennial Christians have become "too smart" to be a part of an ignorant community (church)?

When I think about the number of Millennial Christians, and believers, I have come in contact with, the truth is that many of them are intellectually alive. They are very well read. Most are extremely well spoken. And to the same extent there is a large number of modern believers that have advanced successfully through the academy. With the advances in modern technology, a person who has never been to college still has access to information in the same fashion as the person who matriculates through formal education. The truth is that the local church may stimulate this population's emotions, however there is a remnant of Christians who are seeking something that will take them to a new level of excellence in their moral life and consciousness.

The era of "do it because the Bible says so" is dead. No longer are we able to make this blanket statement with an expectancy to reciprocate a response from modern believers. People are looking for the type of faith that will challenge them into aliveness. People are looking for a place to connect. People are seeking an electrical outlet to resurge their passions surrounding community service and social responsibility. Modern Christians are searching for a place that will enlighten them and challenge them to become moral agents and not just church attendees.

People want to be a part of a faith system that gives them a call to action. People want to belong to a faith system that reproduces the love of Christ out in community. People want to be motivated, and encouraged, to be active participants in the advancement of global change. The title of humanitarian and philanthropist have become ideals for many millennials. I have a friend who doesn't attend church but is committed to giving financially to causes that better the community. People want to make a difference in the world. What they don't want are more sanctuaries and building projects if these projects are not connected to social change. Unfortunately, a small percentage of his money makes it into the church offering plate because of the previous mentioned. He knows his giving won't make it to the causes he is passionate about; therefore he does not give to the local church but to other community organizations. His actions reminds us that people don't just want to feel good on Sunday mornings. People want to connect with the communities they live in. What better feeling does a person get to know they helped improved a social disparity? The personal reward of contributing to community advancement is far greater than knowing you helped the church reach their next tier level on a new sanctuary capital campaign.

By the time complacent Christians reach Wednesday night, they need another pick-me-up from the spiritual high they received on Sunday morning. However, one can observe that some Christians, like my above mentioned friend, remain spiritually high all week because they are connected to something bigger than themselves. They live through helping others live a better life. They feel alive because, at the end of the day, they were able to bring hope to someone who had given up on living. What I have noticed in my years of service is that people who serve with me keep their "high" longer than the Christian who refuses to be involved in community projects. What I mean is when people serve once they become anxious to serve again!

The truth is that people are looking for a more fulfilling walk with God. People are looking for ways to connect with their creator in a way that makes them feel as though they matter. People don't just want to be a part of a church, they want to be a part of a community of believers that are making a noticeable difference in the community. Miguel De La Torre writes that, the life and sayings of Christ, as recognized by the faith community that searches the biblical text for guidance to life's ethical dilemmas, serve as the ultimate standard of morality.[63] In other words we should not seek to study the word of God for the sake of saying that we have become scholars of the text. Instead, the text should illuminate a light within us that challenges us to push past the wrongs of the world with the hope of displaying Christ's love and affection. The bible should not be solely used to make us better Christians; through it we should strive to be better people in general.

Most people can experience, and become overwhelmed by too much worship. I have yet to meet a person who gets overwhelmed about too much service.

Think about it. Ponder and consider with me the religious, and community, environments you frequent. You can ask a person to attend worship with you and their response will either be, "sure", "I've already been", "I have a church home already" or "no". These are the polite answers. Most people have an inclination to answer the invitation with strong consideration after weighing a plethora of options. There are so many other things they have to consider when positioned with this option of how they will spend their time. However, in my experience, in most cases when you ask someone to serve, whether they just returned from a mission's trip in Haiti or not, the answer will often be in the affirmative. Most individuals, even if their words turn out to be lies, have a greater propensity to say "yes" quicker than they would if they were invited to a worship experience.

Does this insinuate that people have the aptitude to pull in the direction of service stronger than they do for worship? If nothing else the person will inquire more about the opportunity instead of giving an automatic decline. This is the reason I always invite people to serve with The Worship Center more than I ask them to come

---

[63] Torre, Miguel A De La. 2004. *Doing Christian Ethics from the Margins.* Maryknoll: Orbis Books.

to one of our many worship environments. Serving keeps people moving. Serving keeps people excited about their Christianity. Serving keeps people involved. Serving gives people responsibilities and makes them accountable for their commitments. Service makes people want to do more and connect with other opportunities; because they feel like they are a part of something that is bigger than themselves.

I remember one commentary writing a very strong critique about to the modern American church. With much respect I have to agree with some of their words. I honestly believe that their sentiments echo the sentiments, and feelings, of many millennials around the globe. They write, "You don't matter. Churches that ignore the world aren't giving us any context for spirituality. Jesus walked in a world with political, social, economic, and spiritual forces at play. We, too, walk in a world with all of these forces. Jesus engaged them."[64] I agree that churches and ministries who don't make the word of God pragmatic and practical don't help the believer maximize their highest potential in their faith walk. We can preach and teach the beatitudes of Christ, as located in the book of Matthew 5:3-11, but if we never reach these communities, outlined in the text, have we truly been obedient to Christ's message?

> [3]God blesses those who are poor and realize their need for him, for the Kingdom of Heaven is theirs. [4]God blesses those who mourn, for they will be comforted. [5]God blesses those who are humble, for they will inherit the whole earth. [6]God blesses those who hunger and thirst for justice, for they will be satisfied. [7]God blesses those who are merciful, for they will be shown mercy. [8]God blesses those whose hearts are pure, for they will see God. [9]God blesses those who work for peace, for they will be called the children of God. [10]God blesses those who are persecuted for doing right, for the Kingdom of Heaven is theirs. [11]God blesses you when people mock you and persecute you and lie about you and say all sorts of evil things against you because you are my followers. [12]Be happy about it! Be very glad!

---

[64] Unknown. 2015. *Here are 3 reasons no one is joining your church (plus one more)*. October 13. www.reluctantxian.wordpress.com/2015/10/13/here-are-3-reasons-no-one-is-joining-your-church-plus-one-more.

For a great reward awaits you in heaven. And remember, the ancient prophets were persecuted in the same way. (Matthew 5:3-12)

The text continues with the admonishment from Jesus himself in that we should be the example and light to these communities in the world:

> [13]You are the salt of the earth. But what good is salt if it has lost its flavor? Can you make it salty again? It will be thrown out and trampled underfoot as worthless. [14]You are the light of the world—like a city on a hilltop that cannot be hidden. [15]No one lights a lamp and then puts it under a basket. Instead, a lamp is placed on a stand, where it gives light to everyone in the house. [16]In the same way, let your good deeds shine out for all to see, so that everyone will praise your heavenly Father. (Matthew 5:13-16)

Are we seeing the connection point between the marginalized, our Christian responsibility and Christ's message? I believe we should engage these human dynamics and groups of people as well. I believe we should be Christians that are actively involved, just like Jesus was, in political, social, economic and spiritual issues. The beatitudes should shape our attitudes about how we serve, give and effect the environments around us. I believe Christians, if no one else, because we profess to have the highest level of moral obligation, should be on the front line to champion certain issues and problems around the globe. The poor, the hurting and the hungry are just a few populations Christ challenges us to engage with. In our modern context this would include the felon, the single parent and the person living with HIV. We no longer become the salt of the earth as it was in Jesus' day. Rather, as described in my culture, we become the Lawry's Seasoned Salt™ for our communities.

Daisaku Ikeda writes that what our world most requires now is the kind of education that fosters love for humankind, that develops character- that provides an intellectual basis for the realization of peace and empowers learners to contribute to and improve society."[65] In our Sunday morning encounters do we excite people or do we empower them to be change agents in the world? Are we simply teaching love or are we nurturing love into the hearts of our attendees? Do we only desire that people contribute to the offering plates of our churches with no expectation for them to give their time, talents and passions to the betterment of humanity? Are we willing to push into a Christian consciousness that runs parallel to Christ's consciousness? Later in this text I will discuss this term and how we should embrace its essence in our daily walk.

There are other trumpets throughout history who sound the same clarion call to all who are willing to listen. We can learn from their lives and examples what obedience to the message of Christ will manifest in our communities. Dr. Martin Luther King reminds us that "We must remember that intelligence is not enough. Intelligence plus character- that is the true goal of education. The complete education gives one not only power of concentration, but worthy objectives upon which to concentrate."[66] Although we may lead churches that have a majority of knowledgeable millennials who attend, we cannot stop with matters of the brain and the mind. We must nurture people who are willing to reach levels of the heart. We must challenge ourselves to take our intellect and marry it to our convictions to serve. We cannot simply focus on knowing more about God if we are unwilling to produce God's presence here on earth.

Dr. King's life gives us but one example of what passion, obedience, courage, and the will to manifest Christ Consciousness can produce. However, he isn't the only one who helps us to shift our views about ministry in context. He isn't the only person

---

[65] Carter, Lawrence Edward, George David Miller, and Neelakanta Radhakrishnan. 2001. *Global Ethical Options*. Trumbull: Weatherhill.

[66] Carter, Lawrence Edward, George David Miller, and Neelakanta Radhakrishnan. 2001. *Global Ethical Options*. Trumbull: Weatherhill.

who spoke up, and spoke out, about issues that others remained silent about. From the voice of Moses to the lyrics of hip hop artist, and lyricist, Kendrick Lamar the message remains consistent: Love God. Love Others.

We have to get to place in our lives where we embrace the history that was presented before us in such a way that we seek to learn from its wisdom. I believe that we are embarking on a time where a shift is preparing to take place in the consciousness of humanity and Christianity. People are changing the way they view religion, spirituality and their personal involvement with the world. Henry R. Halloran, Jr. and Lawrence S. Bale are two other names we can call on to support this evolution of Christ consciousness. For they believe that "humankind is on the threshold of creating and discovering a dialogical vision of global concern and global responsibility that will be embraced by individuals, organizations, nations, and faith communities." [67] Global concern and global responsibility are now walking hand and hand. No longer does the present generation have the sole desire to bring awareness to the issues around the globe. They also want to act to make a difference in the betterment of the globe. I recall a time where social awareness was the harnessing caveat that brought people together.

In these communities of people individuals were brought together because of how they felt regarding the issues that were being brought to the forefront of peoples mind. Social, community and humanitarian awareness is what caused many people to gather for the purpose of thinking through solutions. Today, millennials could care less about think tanks and town hall meetings. What the modern millennial Christian desires is a solution to today's issues that require blood, sweat, tears and the sounding of a strong voice to champion for those who cannot speak for themselves.

---

[67] Carter, Lawrence Edward, George David Miller, and Neelakanta Radhakrishnan. 2001. *Global Ethical Options*. Trumbull: Weatherhill.

We are entering a consciousness of humanity where people see the distresses of the world and seek to take accountability for its reconciliation.

What is happening in the world today is nuptials between the church and the community, Christianity and culture. Finally we are at the turning point in the faith where the church is leaving the building. Mary C. Boys gives us her perception on how there is a relationship between religion and culture. She writes:

> "Does one's commitment of faith lead to any of the following positions: An uncompromising countercultural stance? An acquiescent position, receptive to the categories and claims of one's milieu and desirous of making one's faith "relevant" above all else? A dualistic position, in which one acknowledges the essentially corrupt nature of humankind, yet recognizes both one's 'caughtness' in it and God's sustaining grace? A synthetic position, in which one sees God's rule established in the nature of things and so attempts to reconcile divine and human into one system? A transformist position, in which one seeks to change the world in accord with the values of one's faith?[68]

To simplify, we must be willing to take a position that bucks broken systems. We must be willing to enter into environments that, culturally, others refuse to participate with. If we are going to become more relevant in today's culture we must be willing to do what is necessary to regain this relevancy. This isn't a competition with other religions, or faiths. What we are in opposition with are the non-religious things that take people away from participating in their social, and humanitarian, responsibility. We have to be prepared to dialogue with grace and injustices simultaneously. As I recall one of my college professors telling a young theologian who had just begun his scholarly journey, "you have to be willing to hold the newspaper in one hand and the bible in the other." As religious leaders we have to speak the parables of Christ as well as the problems portrayed throughout the various media outlets. There is a paradigm shift preparing to take place where the sacred and

---

[68] Boys, Mary C. 1989. *Educating in Faith*. Lima: Academic Renewal Press.

the secular prepare to gel. Where people begin to embrace their personal humanity as being both flesh and spirit living in the same consciousness. Where people are guided by a light that transcends the darkness' of this world. The modern millennial Christian seeks to follow the compass of faith in the direction that points toward social, civil and humanitarian transformation. If we are going to reach, and attract, the modern believer and non-believer, there are some critical adjustments that need to be made in how we showcase our belief system out to the world.

The Bible speaks on various occasions about the importance of establishing a strong sense of community with our faith:

> *[1] How wonderful and pleasant it is when brothers live together in harmony! [2] For harmony is as precious as the anointing oil that was poured over Aaron's head, which ran down his beard and onto the border of his robe. [3] Harmony is as refreshing as the dew from Mount Hermon that falls on the mountains of Zion. And there the lord has pronounced his blessing, even life everlasting. (Psalm 133)*

> *[24] Let us think of ways to motivate one another to acts of love and good works. [25] And let us not neglect our meeting together, as some people do, but encourage one another, especially now that the day of his return is drawing near. (Hebrews 10:24-25)*

> *[1] Dear brothers and sisters, if another believer is overcome by some sin, you who are godly should gently and humbly help that person back onto the right path. And be careful not to fall into the same temptation yourself. [2] Share each other's burdens, and in this way obey the law of Christ. [3] If you think you are too important to help someone, you are only fooling yourself. You are not that important. [4] Pay careful attention to your own work, for then you will get the satisfaction of a job well done, and you won't need to compare yourself to anyone else. [5] For we are each responsible for our own conduct. (Galatians 6:1-5)*

Each of these scriptures carry an underline thread of a more perfect world. What we understand is that there will never be a perfect community. However we can strive towards a world that is better than our present. Harmony should be a standard of living we all strive for. It should be our goal to live in such a way with others where all of our actions and intents bring us closer to those around us. Love and good works are the foundation for manifesting this into our present reality. Mary Boys also gives us a critical model to consider if we are going to properly evangelize to the millennial. This model, in my opinion us undergirded by the above mentioned scriptures. She outlines the following as things to consider:

1. **Revelation**- Primacy of revelation accorded to scripture

2. **Conversion**- Conversion of the affections stressed 'A change of heart, not of opinion'

3. **Faith & Belief**- Faith developed from one's experiential knowledge

4. **Faith and Culture**- Distinction made between supernatural and natural

5. **Goal of Education**- To deepen one's personal conversion

6. **Knowledge**- Spiritual knowledge unified thinking, feeling, and action.[69]

If I can, I would like to further engage with her ideas and provide some biblical, and modern day context for her recommendations. As it relates to **Revelation** there are countless ways that we can utilize the biblical text as our compass for service and faith. What the scripture offers us, is a roadmap of things to consider which have been tested for centuries by generations before us. From the days of Abraham, to modern day, much of what we need to guide us is located in a text that has been preserved for well over 2000 years. It's primacy does not come solely with the fact that these words are from God, but also the point that these words have been able to be applied throughout the course of history.

With regard to the practice of **Conversion,** we see introduced the idea that true change takes place at the core level of the heart and soul. This is why David writes in Psalm 51:10, *"Create in me a clean heart, O God. Renew a loyal spirit within me."*. While this text contextually referred to David's repentance after the prophet Nathan

---

[69] Boys, Mary C. 1989. *Educating in Faith*. Lima: Academic Renewal Press.

brought to his attention his adulterous relationship with Bathsheba, we can echo these same words as they relate to our relationship with the world around us.

The distinction between **Faith and Belief** must be identified for the millennial believer and curious faith practitioner. What Boys points out is that it is only through our personal experience that these two things are nurtured. If faith and belief are fostered through our experiences then we should be encouraging individuals to get out and engage their faith with the world.

Boys also points out that there is a paralleling relationship between **Faith and Culture.** As we have discussed previously in this text, there is a distinction between the spiritual and the natural. However, we must understand that they operate under the same cosmos. In the same regard we need not separate belief and community. We should apprehend that they too operate under the same experience.

With that we should have a clear direction as to the **Goal of Education.** Each individual has their own method of learning. Similarly, the goals associated with our walk with God and involvement with the community must be customized to our personalities.

Taking this into consideration, **Knowledge**, in my opinion, is the first step to enlightenment. The more we know about the world around us the greater our awareness becomes regarding humanitarian issues. Equally the more we know, and discover, about ourselves the more we begin to realize our personal responsibility in the world's advancement.

Mary Boys and the modern millennial would agree with Harrison Elliott in that:
> Elliott was not opposed to utilizing the Bible in Sunday schools or to worship that sought "direct experience of God," but he felt both

Bible study and worship had to be brought to bear on present experience and reinterpreted in light of contemporary problems, lest they were merely interesting or consoling rather than pertinent to modern life: Bible study and prayer and worship will not of themselves produce vital religious experience. It is only when these are utilized because of a concern for human life and because of a sense of need for resources beyond those which seem available in human endeavor that they lead to the vitalizing of religious experience.[70]

The words of Boys echo in the ears of modern Christians in that they seek the type of faith that challenges them to be better people in the world. We can no longer study the word of God for the sake of studying. We can no longer pray to our creator for the purpose of a general conversation. We can no longer attend worship for the purpose of having our names crossed off the list for attendance. At some point, the modern Christian wants to take what is learned, and taught, and create practical application out of it. The word of God has to be made relevant to our current experiences and happenings. What we study has to be lived and executed. The depth of our prayers must reach the ears of God with the concerns of the world. We can no longer ask people to pray and read God's word if we do not introduce a human concern that can be effected through our prayers and God's word.

Mary Boys is also on point with her synopsis on how the modern millennial perceives the church universal as an educational enterprise:

1. **Revelation**- Revelation is found in social interaction

2. **Conversion**- Viewed primarily as growth

3. **Faith and Belief**- Religious experience more important than dogma and creedal formulas

4. **Theology**- Modern biblical criticism used

5. **Faith and culture**- The sacred and the secular are essentially harmonious

---

[70] Boys, Mary C. 1989. *Educating in Faith*. Lima: Academic Renewal Press.

6. **Goal of Education**- The reconstruction of society

7. **Knowledge**- Attention to the link between theory and practice

8. **Social Sciences**- Interest in social science outweighed interest in theology

9. **Curriculum & Teaching**- Curriculum more inclusive and humanistic

10. **Education as Political**- Social reform and educational form linked.[71]

Much of what she says still has strong relevancy in today's consciousness of modern millennials. She is right in that most people find their purpose in social engagement. It is not until people get out and see the pains of the world that they become more empathetic to the hurts of others. This new consciousness is a result of people interacting with other people and environments that are other than their own. It is not until we are, as Paul notes in Roman's 12:1, "Transformed by the renewing of the mind" that we can truly experience personal growth. It is not until our consciousness changes that we are able to see clear our purpose in today's world. As it relates to our faith and belief, it will be our interactions with the world, and not with the church itself, that will strengthen these two character traits.

The modern millennial would like offer a strong critique on the biblical text. I agree that a 5000 year old text should be examined to accentuate its relevancy in today's world. The contemporary Christian, with wisdom, should not throw the baby out with the bath water (as my grandmother would say). But rather cherish the principles and morals the baby represents throughout the text with the hope of making the baby comfortable in the tub we call present time. The truth, as Boys points out, is that this baby has to fit, and balance, in a world of both sacred and secular consciousness's. No longer can we place the bible in the spiritual world with no regard

---

[71] Boys, Mary C. 1989. *Educating in Faith*. Lima: Academic Renewal Press.

for how it effects and shapes the carnal. We must understand that the power of God's word has, as Boys suggests, the power to reconstruct society and cultures. It has the potential to shift the paradigms of the world for those who chose to adopt its value and principles. It becomes of unexplainable value when the bridge is built between what 'God says' and what 'man manifests through God's word'. Imagine a world, if you would, where people were inspired to create God's word and not just read God's word.

The word of God has the potential to bridge the gap between the social sciences, humanities and theology. The biblical text addresses many, if not all, of the issues and questions that plague humanity today. How is this possible? The issues we face today are not new but have been around since the beginning of time. Genocide, poverty, incarceration, murder, racism, sexism, classism, and oppression, to name a few, have all shown their faces in the cultures before us. The bible has proven to be a great standard for addressing and understanding how to work through these social dynamics. What it has taught us, as Boys points out, is that we have to take an inclusive approach to how we exercise our theology and understanding of God today. We have to embrace the notion that God does not want to stay in the church alone. Therefore, we must be willing to include God in the various components of the world. However, as Boys concludes, each of these points must focus us in the direction of personal enlightenment and social change.

Henri Nouwen is another scholar whose words I chose to review as a speaker for the modern millennial. What he mentions in his book *"The Wounded Healer: Ministry in Contemporary Society"* is a true depiction of what is happening in the world of ministry and church. He says that, "When we feel ourselves unable to relate to the Christian message, we may wonder whether this is not due to the fact that, for many people, Christianity has become an ideology. When Christianity is reduced to an all-encompassing ideology, those of us who live in the modern age are all too prone to be skeptical about its relevance to our life experience."[72] Nouwen only echoes what Boys states previously in that the modern Christian wants an experience with God and the world; and not just with God and the church. What we can note about his words are that he also has a concern about the relevancy of Christianity and religion in the world. What he points out is that people need a message that they can relate to. He mentions that we cannot only accept the idea of God, but that we should strive to see God's presence manifested in our communities. To the same consideration, we should be striving as Christians to reveal God's presence to others through our life experiences. I would suggest that the focal point of his statement is that relevancy and relationship work together.

It is vastly important that we begin to hear the concerns and criticisms of today's spiritual practitioner. It is imperative, for the sake of Christianity and the faith, that we approach relevancy as a key component for sustainability. We have to embrace the truth that faith has held together humanity for centuries and generations before us. We must be clear in knowing that the importance of faith and belief in God, and God's involvement in the world, shapes humanity and it's advancement. As we look out into the world we can observe that when people lose hope and love their actions reflect what they believe.

Instead of operating in love, hope, grace and peace they begin to operate in anger, fear, misguided ignorance and sin. Nouwen further states in his text that, "Here people become aware that the choice is no longer between our present world or a better world, but between a new world or no world."[73] When people are consistently asking the questions, "Where is God?" and "Why is God allowing this?" we must step

---

[72] Nouwen, Henri J. M. 1972. *The Wounded Healer: Ministry in Contemporary Society*. New York: Doubleday Religion.

[73] Nouwen, Henri J. M. 1972. *The Wounded Healer: Ministry in Contemporary Society*. New York: Doubleday Religion.

back and re-evaluate our involvement in the answers to these concerns. We must begin to ask ourselves the questions, "Will I be the change I seek to see in the world?" and "Am I willing to do my best to create the environments I seek to see in the world?" We must be willing to revisit the biblical text where God asks a man of his responsibility for the life of his brother:

> *8One day Cain suggested to his brother, "Let's go out into the fields." And while they were in the field, Cain attacked his brother, Abel, and killed him. 9Afterward the lord asked Cain, "Where is your brother? Where is Abel?" "I don't know," Cain responded. "Am I my brother's guardian?" 10But the lord said, "What have you done? Listen! Your brother's blood cries out to me from the ground!" (Genesis 4:8-10)*

We must be willing to address the issues, the facts and the feelings that are associated with the injustices that continue to happen around the world. However, we cannot simply address these mentioned items. We must also be willing to act in order to reconcile these issues with our current reality. It should be our attempt to create better people. As a result, a better world will begin to manifest itself as the byproduct of people who have become fully aware of themselves and their responsibilities in creating this better world. We cannot be advocates unless we are courageous enough to add value to the environments we frequent. We are the keepers and guardians of those who are unable to protect themselves against the systems, and mindsets, which plague our world.

Henri Nouwen says it best when he writes, "Their goal is not a better human being, but a new human being; one who relates to the self and the world in ways which are still explored but which belong to our hidden potentials."[74] We ultimately must be willing to create and cultivate a new type of Christian and religious practitioner. We should be striving to awaken the fullest potential of those who walk through our church doors. We cannot become what millennials have assumed about

---

[74] Nouwen, Henri J. M. 1972. *The Wounded Healer: Ministry in Contemporary Society.* New York: Doubleday Religion.

the church. There are so many hidden talents and gifts that can, and should, be used for the advancement of the kingdom of God here on earth. Unfortunately, these assets will never reach their highest potential until relevancy enters the minds of those we seek to get involved. We must be courageous enough to answer the question for the millennial, "why should I give you my time, talent and tenth?"

If Christianity and the church are going to regain relevancy in humanity it must be open to the critiques of modern millennial believers and potential believers. It must see the world as they see it. It must value the things this community values. It must appreciate the gifts and talents this generation is willing to bring. However, it must also understand that these gifts and talents do not want to stay bound in the four walls of our church buildings. Nouwen is correct when he makes his observation about the consciousness of the modern millennial. He writes, "They live by the vision of a new world and refuse to be sidetracked by trivial ambitions of the moment. Thus they transcend their present condition and move from a passive fatalism to a radical activism."[75] We must understand that the modern Christian seeks to create a more perfect world. What they seek are opportunities to create this world without the red tape of church politics and denominational hindrances and approvals. The colors of the altar dressings matter not to the millennial. They could care less if purple, red, white or green is draped upon the front of the worship center. What they do care about are the colors we paint on the walls of buildings that have been left vacant to drug dealers and homeless persons. This generation, as we have noticed in present media, does not take a passive approach to addressing any social issue. They are willing to voice their concerns, and opinions, at the risk be being unpopular for the sake of community change. As churches, ministries and contemporary Christians we too must be willing to be unpopular for the sake of leading what that change will look like.

---

[75] Nouwen, Henri J. M. 1972. *The Wounded Healer: Ministry in Contemporary Society.* New York: Doubleday Religion.

WHAT IS GOD TELLING BELIEVERS AND NON-BELIEVERS?

Humanity is listening for the heartbeat of God. There are various communities that are searching for the existence of God here on earth. There are countless people who are looking for hope in the community from the church as well as the Christian faith. Humanity is seeking God's presence here on earth. Humanity wants to feel the pulse of generosity and kindness present in the everyday happenings of life. There are people who are searching for the Christian community to stand up and make its presence known in the blueprint of community service and care. Humanity is looking for a moral example of right living and selfless care. People are looking in the direction of the church, and Christianity, for the answers to complex questions about the happenings of the world. Humanity wants to connect to the heart of God. As we discussed in the previous chapter, millennials are in search of ways to connect to the community while simultaneously fulfilling their religious obligation. True Christians should have the desire to be the heartbeat of God. What is God telling the believer and the non-believer? To BE who we were created to BE: Servants to humanity and champions for community change.

History continues to unfold itself. To the same degree history continues to repeat itself. In the words of Solomon we can learn how to view this consciousness we call life now:

> [2]"Everything is meaningless," says the Teacher, "completely meaningless!" [3]What do people get for all their hard work under the

sun? ⁴Generations come and generations go, but the earth never changes. ⁵The sun rises and the sun sets, then hurries around to rise again. ⁶The wind blows south, and then turns north. Around and around it goes, blowing in circles. ⁷Rivers run into the sea, but the sea is never full. Then the water returns again to the rivers and flows out again to the sea. ⁸Everything is wearisome beyond description. No matter how much we see, we are never satisfied. No matter how much we hear, we are not content. ⁹History merely repeats itself. It has all been done before. Nothing under the sun is truly new. ¹⁰Sometimes people say, "Here is something new!" But actually it is old; nothing is ever truly new. ¹¹We don't remember what happened in the past, and in future generations, no one will remember what we are doing now. (Ecclesiastes 1:2-11)

Solomon reminds us that there is nothing new under the sun. Solomon places our actions into perspective by saying that what we do means nothing in the grand scale of God's larger plan for the world. As he closes this specific periscope of text he also mentioned the truth that very little of what we do now will be remembered. The caveat to this statement is that we won't be remembered if we don't do things that matter for humanity. One certainty is that history continues to repeat the disparities of humankind. The disparities we see today are the same disparities that have been present sense the beginning of time. What we can observe is that history continues to repeat the cycle of oppression, classism, sexism, racism, health disparities, educational divides, economic disparities, environmental and climate changes, sexual equality and countless other issues that continue to plague our world. It continues to repeat economic inequality.

However, with the repetition of all things mentioned, something else simultaneously repeats itself. The cries of children who have become victims of sex trafficking. The cries of people living with HIV who have been outcast by their families and society. The cries of felons who are looking for a fresh start in society. The cries of humanity for world peace and a better life for all mankind. While history repeats itself with disparity and the above mentioned issues, humanity continues to cry out for hope. Humanity wants to hear the heartbeat of God in the world.

What we must understand is that it is easy to be the hands and feet of God. With modern technology and resources, there is nothing complicated with community service. It is easy to do service related activities on behalf of God. It is simple to connect with multiple organizations and nonprofits that are leading the way to create change and liberation in our local and global communities. There is nothing that holds back a local church in Atlanta from connecting to a ministry in the Ghana to build a water purification system in that area. It has become easy to give, and to serve, whether local or internationally, spontaneously. There are countless opportunities that people can connect with and not be directly connected to the organization. The doors are open. This is one practice that we pride ourselves in at The Worship Center. You do not need to be a member, or a connector as we call them, at our church to serve with us in our five partnership projects.

It is easy for a person to motivate and excite another person to give. What I have observed over my course in ministry is that communities inspire other communities. It is the work that every day people do that inspire others to make a difference. It is the call, and challenge, from the local barbershop owner that mobilizes people. The modern millennial has no concern for who they serve with as long as they are serving. What they realize is that service has no boundaries. But how many True Christians will make it a point to adopt service as a lifestyle? We can no longer make service opportunities synonymous with church work. How many modern millennial Christians will push themselves to serve on more occasions than just Thanksgiving and Christmas? (The two major times of the year where we can observe an influx of community service and work.) The truth of the matter is the heartbeat of God should have a consistent sound in humanity; displayed by the actions of True Christians worldwide all year long.

There is a pulse in life. Everything we experience has a beat and a thump associated with it. We are all connected to the rhythm of life. The key to experiencing life is connecting to that underline rhythmic thrust that keeps the world turning. The same way in which blood flows through the heart of the human body, humanitarian acts should pour through the DNA of the globe. When we see the world we should see the manifestation of Christ's words being manifested in the world. In today's culture we should be the word of God, as flesh, in our experience. We should observe, first hand, the words of Jesus coming to light in our culture. Every continent, every community, every class, every family, every gender, every human is connected, in some way, to this web of the world. The common Disney™ phrase of "It's a small world after all" is an understatement.

We are all universally connected. One element of Christ Consciousness, as we are prepared to uncover and define, is to understand that we are all linked to a larger cosmic energy; God. We have to acknowledge that there is something greater than ourselves that is controlling the happenings of the world. We must be clear that we are only a piece of the universe's consciousness of what it is and how it seeks to expand itself. We are only agents of change and not the change agent itself. At whatever point in history this text is being read, I can guarantee there is a pulse in the world. There is something that is calling for the attention of the church and the Christian faith.

Just because we plug our ears with the headphones of today, does not entail that the cries of our community have ceased. We cannot continue to turn a deaf hear to the pleas of the communities we have been called to serve. Maybe the pulse is directing our attention to police brutality and murder. Maybe the pulse is directing our attention to the political campaigns and government agendas. Maybe the pulse is directing our attention to the lack of food in Somalia. Maybe the pulse is directing our attention towards international terrorism. Maybe the pulse is making us aware that racism and prejudice still exist in our communities. Maybe the pulse is drawing our attention to the lack of clean running water in Ghana. Perhaps the pulse is drawing our attention to the terroristic actions of a group of people abroad. Maybe the pulse has us aware that health services, a basic human right, is not offered to all of humanity. Regardless of time, there is a pulse present.

Although, in the book by Dean Lawrence Carter, *Global Ethical Options*, there are 20 ethical principles, which I will, and have highlighted through this text; there are a few I would love to highlight in the context of what I believe God wants to communicate to the believer and the nonbeliever; the ability to 1. Transcend tribalism and embrace globalism, 2. Take individual responsibility, 3. Create an ideal of community, society, or culture, 4. Include devotion to community and 5. Practice coherence.[76]

Let us dig deeper into these concepts. To **transcend tribalism and embrace globalism** is to rid ourselves of the idea that smaller communities are not a part of the larger community called humanity. Christians must leave the "my church" and "our ministry" mentality and begin to speak the reality of "we can collectively". While we may differ in polity, practice and pragmatic views, the truth is that the world needs to experience the love of God regardless of how it is executed. We cannot continue to build small tribes of people in an effort to prove whose individual method works effectively. Instead we should clinch globalism as our perspective when creating community initiatives. The world will not become a better place if we continue to create isolated sects of people who don't have a global perspective on service.

To take individual responsibility would entail that we accept our part in making the world a better place. For, according to the biblical text, we will be held accountable for our personal part in humanity's self-actualization. Galatians 6:4-5 reads, "But let each one test his own work, and then his reason to boast will be in

---

[76] Carter, Lawrence Edward, George David Miller, and Neelakanta Radhakrishnan. 2001. *Global Ethical Options*. Trumbull: Weatherhill.

himself alone and not in his neighbor. For each will have to bear his own load." The root of this passage of scripture points us in the consciousness that each of us has a portion of the load to carry. We all share in carrying the burdens associated with humanitarian service. As Christians we should own our part in making the world a better, more loving, place. Imagine what could be accomplished if 100 people took 1% of individual responsibility at ending homelessness in their city; I can guarantee a 100% success rate!

To create an ideal of community, society or culture simply means that we create a standard for right living and that we adopt the moral compass that the bible provides. As we have previously mentioned in this text, it is the ethics and principles of a person that guides their actions. If we can connect personal standards to personal responsibility the world would begin to become a better place. When we as Christians begin to approach our faith from a holistic point of view we will be able to expand our reach to those who need the love of Christ most. We must be willing to make serving others a walk of life and not a solitary event in which we choose when, how and in what capacity we would like to be used.

To include devotion to community would mean that the same fervency we have for Sunday morning worship should carry over into our desire to be involved in the public. The same commitment we have for ensuring our attendance to national conferences and convocations should carry over into our commitment to answer in the affirmative when called upon to serve. As true Christians we must remain fervent and zealous to manifesting the message of Christ during our consciousness called life. We cannot quit when resources are low. We cannot stop when the message appears to be falling on deaf ears. We cannot cease from serving when we notice the statistics rising. We must remain devoted when times are difficult and when obstacles arise.

Finally to practice coherence would entail us embracing the consciousness that all things we do are connected. What happens in Texas effects those who live in Thailand. How we help people with HIV in Baltimore will encourage the movement of ending the epidemic in Sub-Saharan African. When we move to end childhood illiteracy in Atlanta something begins to happen in the consciousness of those in Asia.

I have always been the trumpet to speak my belief in that we are co-creators with God. I have always believed that God uses humans to manifest His will and desires here on earth. I have always seen, first hand, how God chooses humans to create a more perfect world. From the beginning of time God has used man, and woman, to be change agents here on earth. According to history, God has not only been working through us but also with us. We become God's fellow workers, according to Martin Buber, by making peace and helping bring about world peace. Each time we connect with other communities, we are destined and summoned by God to do so.[77] It is more than just an internal feeling we have to help others. Rather, there is a magnetic pull from the ultimate energy we call God that tugs us in the direction to do well towards others. It is God placing a "HELP WANTED" sign on the continents of the globe requesting people who are willing to help make a difference. God is searching for people who will work locally, and people who are willing to go great distances, to spread peace to communities who face daily turmoil and hopelessness. God is calling people who are unafraid to come close to Him by looking into the eyes of the oppressed and the marginalized. As we discussed earlier in this text, to look in the eyes of these communities is to also stare into the eyes of God.

Aristotle offers three things to consider when he says, "The agent also must be in a certain condition when he does them; in the first place he must have the

---

[77] Buber, Martin. 1970. *I and Thou*. New York: Klaus Reprint.

knowledge, secondly he must choose the acts, and choose them for their own sakes, and thirdly his actions must proceed from a firm and unchangeable character."[78] I would add that knowledge, or the act of knowing, is only the beginning to our quest of becoming change agents for God. What we have highlighted in this text are various facts that would strengthen a person's knowledge about the social and global issues happening around us. However, as Solomon's life becomes a prime example for us, wisdom must be introduced into the equation. We cannot simply know what is right and wrong. We cannot merely know what actions to take. We must be wise in taking what we have learned and seek God's guidance to execute our actions wisely. Let us recall the moment in history when Solomon became the world's wisest man:

> *At Gibeon the LORD appeared to Solomon in a dream by night, and God said, "Ask what I shall give you." And Solomon said, "You have shown great and steadfast love to your servant David my father, because he walked before you in faithfulness, in righteousness, and in uprightness of heart toward you. And you have kept for him this great and steadfast love and have given him a son to sit on his throne this day. And now, O LORD my God, you have made your servant king in place of David my father, although I am but a little child. I do not know how to go out or come in. And your servant is in the midst of your people whom you have chosen, a great people, too many to be numbered or counted for multitude. Give your servant therefore an understanding mind to govern your people, that I may discern between good and evil, for who is able to govern this your great people?" It pleased the Lord that Solomon had asked this. And God said to him, "Because you have asked this, and have not asked for yourself long life or riches or the life of your enemies, but have asked for yourself understanding to discern what is right, behold, I now do according to your word. Behold, I give you a wise and discerning mind, so that none like you has been before you and none like you shall arise after you. (1 Kings 3:5-12)*

Secondly, Aristotle states that we must choose what we do solely for the sake of doing them because it is right to do. The biblical text encourages us in the same regard that we should not be tired in doing good and serving others because it is God's will for us to do them. Paul writes, "And let us not grow weary of doing good, for in due season we will reap, if we do not give up." (Galatians 6:9) True Christians

---

[78] Aristotle. 1997. *Nichomachean Ethics.* London: Wordsworth.

do not serve because they want Christian brownie points. They do not serve because they feel obligated to. They do not serve to fulfill their community service assessment for the association. True Christians serve because they understand that it is their response to the call of God on their lives. I believe the reaping Paul talks about in this text has nothing to do with personal gain. If I could place this scripture in the context of humanity service it would read "And let the world not grow fatigued in doing the work of Christ or displaying Christ's love on others. For after time has taken its course we will see a change because of our actions in response to God's challenge, and summons, in our lives."

Finally Aristotle says that our actions have to be rooted in our individual consistent character. The bible mentions that there are a few character traits that we should all consider adopting. I agree that the items mentioned below would assist us in our ethical ideals, and standards, towards helping others with genuine intentions. Paul writes,

> "Put on then, as God's chosen ones, holy and beloved, compassionate hearts, kindness, humility, meekness, and patience, bearing with one another and, if one has a complaint against another, forgiving each other; as the Lord has forgiven you, so you also must forgive. And above all these put on love, which binds everything together in perfect harmony. And let the peace of Christ rule in your hearts, to which indeed you were called in one body. And be thankful." (Colossians 3:12-15)

This small list of ideals and character traits proves as a great ethical road map that places us on the right path to doing the work of Christ with pure intentions. If we were to adopt just a few of these ideals the world would instantly become a better place. If we could perfect a couple of these character traits we would strengthen our ability to be change agents in the world. I would be remised if I did not point out the consistent trait that is evident in this particular scripture, as well as in this text: Love. As the author acknowledges, this trait binds all the other character traits together. So I would recommend that we begin with perfecting our love towards others, and humanity, as a point of departure for becoming better change agents. As we are beginning to notice, love is the common fiber for re-establishing church and Christian relevancy. What we are noticing is that to express love is to express the presence of God on earth.

Henri Nouwen supports this idea when he writes that, "His appearance in our midst has made it undeniably clear that changing the human heart and changing human society are not separate tasks, but are as interconnected as the two beams of the cross."[79] What we do for Christ, on behalf of God, and for others are all connected to one another. We must be conscious in our attempts to remain cognizant of this truth.

---

[79] Nouwen, Henri J. M. 1972. *The Wounded Healer: Ministry in Contemporary Society*. New York: Doubleday Religion.

CHRISTIANS AS ACTIVE HUMAN AGENTS IN HUMANITY

Medical studies say blood will always flow to the areas of the body that need the greatest attention. Where will the service of Christians flow in blood stream of humanity?

The problem I see with most modern American Christians is instead of being selfless they have become self-serving. This growing group of Christians get excited about building buildings, church anniversaries, Pastor Anniversaries and launching satellite locations, but won't show their support or presence to Town Hall meetings about HIV, community summits surrounding sex trafficking, open forum to address law enforcement brutality or open their facilities for homeless services. It is a sad state of affair that we have seen this transition to a self-centered community only a few generations after the early Christian church. As I mentioned earlier, the early church focused their efforts on building the environments around them. What can be observed of some churches today is the complete opposite; they have separated themselves from the communities in which their four walls are erected. The love of God wants to flow, but there could possibly be a blood clot in the body of Christ.

Have we forgotten the message and model of Jesus?

[35]Then James and John, the sons of Zebedee, came over and spoke to him. "Teacher," they said, "We want you to do us a favor." [36]"What is your request?" he asked. [37]They replied, "When you sit on your glorious throne, we want to sit in places of honor next to you, one on your right and the other on your left." [38]But Jesus said to them, "You don't know what you are asking! Are you able to drink from the bitter cup of suffering I am about to drink? Are you able to be baptized with the baptism of suffering I must be baptized with?" [39]"Oh yes," they replied, "We are able!" Then Jesus told them, "You will indeed drink from my bitter cup and be baptized with my baptism of suffering. [40]But I have no right to say who will sit on my right or my left. God has prepared those places for the ones he has chosen." [41]When the ten other disciples heard what James and John had asked, they were indignant. [42]So Jesus called them together and said, "You know that the rulers in this world lord it over their people, and officials flaunt their authority over those under them. [43]But among you it will be different. Whoever wants to be a leader among

you must be your servant, [44]and whoever wants to be first among you must be the slave of everyone else. [45]For even the Son of Man came not to be served but to serve others and to give his life as a ransom for many." (Mark 10:35-45)

Often times I think to myself that if Jesus were alive today how would He view Christians and our actions to keep His message alive? Would Jesus be pleased with the level of work we are doing in the local community and around the world? Would Jesus recognize His message in the actions that we produce on a day to day basis? How would Jesus feel about the world's mindset of entitlement and narcissism? Would Jesus call out the fact that we have become self-absorbed and not Christ absorbed? Jesus, of all people, was the Son of God. If anyone in history should have had a narcissistic bone in His body it would have been Jesus. If society should have treated anyone with royal treatment, Jesus would have been the prime candidate.

Yet when we look at the model and ministry of Jesus we don't see him sitting at the head of the table too often. Very seldom do we find Jesus hanging out with "his type" of people. Never in the biblical text does Jesus ask for, or require, special treatment based on his connection and relationship with God the father. Jesus never makes himself greater than the everyday person He came in contact with. Where we often find Jesus is sitting on the floors of people's houses having an everyday meal. We often find Jesus in the streets and in the fields in conversation with those who needed His presence most. The fact remains that much of the conflict surrounding Jesus was based on the element that he DID NOT solicit the royal treatment some thought He deserved.

There were countless people in his environment who acknowledged Him as the son of God but could not understand why he refused to accept the title of King of the Jews. Yet many modern Christians have made their walk with Christ an observation sport. They have taken the seat of the King and expect others to do the work Christ challenged us to do. There are many modern Christians who watch the world decay, yet have no conviction in their role for its deterioration. We see countless protests and complaints about the conditions of our communities, yet see very few of these complainers out doing the work needed to rectify these disparities. The Jesus model was a method that touched the weaknesses of society and brought strength to the broken hearted. The model Jesus laid before us was the perfect map to take us to the Promised Land. As we have discovered in this text, Jesus' message sounds as a clear voice, and direction, to what the world needs today.

What modern irrelevant Christians have done is taken that model and packaged the message for "Religious Recruitment". They have a gift of manipulating people with the emotions of Jesus' message with no intent to spread the primary emotion of love throughout the world. Many modern day Christians, and traditional churches, have mastered bringing people in, but have failed in placing a wedge in the revolving door of the church.

What we can learn from the life of Jesus is that God's heartbeat can only be heard if we place our service in the noisy environments of the marginalized. There are communities of people who are listening past the stereotypes and statistics in search for the word of God in their lives. It is not merely in the "still small voice" that God makes His presence known to the world. We should not be searching solely for an audible sound from God to indicate His presence here on earth. We do not always need to hear from the Pastor or preacher to tell us what God is saying or what God is doing in humanity. In some cases it is in those "still small actions" that awaken the consciousness of others to know that God is still present on earth. It is in what we do for the world around us that helps verify that God is working through us and with us in the quest for a better world. Amidst the calamities of society, it's the small random acts of kindness and service that help others receive hope in a better world.

One of the key elements I believe modern Christians are unwilling to swallow, with the responsibility of service, is the aspect of becoming a "ransom for many" as mentioned in the previous text. As a Lead Pastor who is leading the charge for more Christians in service to humanity, I can attest to the discomfort of being that ransom. I can confirm the heartache, fear and ostracism associated with this courageous stance. By definition a ransom is a 'value put up in place for the freedom of something else'. What I believe the author was attempting to communicate in this passage of scripture is that we must be willing to put something on the line at the expense to offer liberty to someone outside of ourselves. Personal sacrifice is at the heart of human service. We must be courageous enough to risk something for the betterment of humanity.

The main object, in my opinion, is personal comfortability. True Christians understand service requires personal time. Serving requires personal resources. Serving requires getting out of the comfort of a warm bed to serve the homeless population on a snowy night in Chicago. Serving requires your phone to ring at 1am to hear the voice of a teenager who wants to get out of the sex trade industry. Serving requires going to the first interview with a felon in order to vouch for their integrity and character. Serving requires going to the non-tourist communities of the Dominican Republic to build a clean water system for the underserved villages.

We must understand that our relationship with others is indicative of our relationship with God. How we respond to the needs of the world allows others to peep into our personal devotion to God. When people see Christians acting Christ like they can make the valid assumption that their association with God, and the gospel message, is motivated by the works and inspiration of Jesus Christ. As Miguel De La Torre states in his text *Doing Christian Ethics from the Margins*, "Right relationship with God is possible only if people act justly toward each other."[80] How can we profess to love and serve God if we are not willing to love and serve others? We cannot continue to separate the level in which we worship from the level in which we serve and love humanity. The bible also speaks the same sentiment as it relates to our relationship with God and our fellow person:

> [7]Dear friends, let us continue to love one another, for love comes from God. Anyone who loves is a child of God and knows God. [8]But anyone who does not love does not know God, for God is love. [9]God showed how much he loved us by sending his one and only Son into the world so that we might have eternal life through him. [10]This is real love—not that we loved God, but that he loved us and sent his Son as a sacrifice to take away our sins. [11]Dear friends, since God loved us that much, we surely ought to love each other. [12]No one has ever seen God. But if we love each other, God lives in us, and his love is brought to full expression in us. [13]And God has given us his Spirit as proof that we live in him and he in us. [14]Furthermore, we have seen with our own eyes and now testify that the Father sent his Son to be the Savior of the world. [15]All who declare that Jesus is the Son of God have God living in them, and they live in God. [16]We know how much God loves us, and we have put our trust in his love. . God is love, and all who live in love live in God, and God lives in them. [17]And as we live in God, our love grows more perfect. So we will not be afraid on the day of judgment, but we can face him with confidence because we live like Jesus here in this world. [18]Such love has no fear, because perfect love expels all fear. If we are afraid, it is for fear of punishment, and this shows that we have not fully experienced his perfect love. [19]We love each other because he loved us first. [20]If someone says, "I love God," but hates a fellow believer, that person is a liar; for if we don't love people we can see, how can we love God, whom we cannot see? [21]And he has given us this command: Those who love God must also love their fellow believers. (1 John 4:7-20)

We must be aware that God has a desire to be a part of our human experiences and encounters. We should know by now that God wants to manifest

---

[80] Torre, Miguel A De La. 2004. *Doing Christian Ethics from the Margins.* Maryknoll: Orbis Books.

His love and His grace through us. We have to share the message with others that God is not a faraway God or a being that sits high and looks down on humanity. This is a comforting aspect for those who feel unassured in their connection with God. Showing God on earth helps people to know they are not alone in this existence we call life. When we show the love of Christ we offer a level of encouragement to those who feel lost and forgotten. To the person who can't depend on the empirical elements of life what we can offer them is hope through the love we display through our actions. Miguel continues to write that, "God does not stand aloof from human experiences, but rather enfleshes Godself in the concrete events of human history. Not only do we learn from the gospel how to be Christ-like, but God, through the Christ event, "learns" how to be human-like.[81]" Through Jesus we see how God manages the weight of being human. Through Jesus we are able to see how divine love manifests itself as agape (or brotherly) love for one another.

Through this example the words located in John 3:16 take root in a very different consciousness. *[16]"For this is how God loved the world: He gave his one and only Son, so that everyone who believes in him will not perish but have eternal life."* The foundation of this text lets us know that God's love was meant for all. This text gives us the truth that God's desire was to be felt and experienced by all who would accept His gift of divine love. God shows that, He too, is willing to give a personal sacrifice at the expense of another's freedom and liberty. This text illustrates that what we do, and how we care, for humanity (the world) will define the condition (to perish or not to perish) of our individual communities.

As mentioned before, we must be willing to take personal responsibility for the condition of our world amid the positions and stances others have taken around us. We must be willing to go alone and become the trendsetters for community change

---

[81] Torre, Miguel A De La. 2004. *Doing Christian Ethics from the Margins.* Maryknoll: Orbis Books.

and Christian responsibility. We must be willing to stand while others are sitting and courageous enough to speak when others are silent. We must be crazy enough to blaze trails and create paths for future generations to follow. We cannot be afraid to go against the status quo but should be open to risking personal gain and our reputations at the expense of global transformation and revolution. Gandhi says that there are moments in your life when you must act, even though you cannot carry your best friends with you. The 'still small voice' within you must always be the final arbiter when there is a conflict of duty.[82] What Gandhi seeks to communicate to us is the message of action as a result of conscious responsibility. What we do should not be contingent on another. Our response should not be the result of man's challenge to do right. Instead we should be following God's word as our primary conciliator to do right because it is the right thing to do.

We must be willing to work as one in our quest for a better world. From the beginning of time to present day we have seen where communities of people have come together in order to create social change. From the days of Moses and Joshua, to the era of Martin King and Malcolm X, it has been proven that when people come together with a shared objective revolutions and liberation takes place. What we can also learn from these champions in history is that when our faith is connected to our actions a surge of energy accompanies our work. This energy, in my opinion, can be defined as God. The force behind what we do should be the same guiding force that challenged our history's leaders to lead the revolutions of their era. According to Dean Lawrence Carter, "The highest form of spirituality is cooperation, the foundation for community."[83] If we are going to create societies that are for the well-being of others we have to work as one on this goal. If we are going to end homelessness and poverty

---

[82] Kripalani, Krishna. 2004. *Mahatma Gandhi: All Men Are Brothers Autobiographical Reflections.* New York: The Continuum International Publishing Group.

[83] Carter, Lawrence Edward, George David Miller, and Neelakanta Radhakrishnan. 2001. *Global Ethical Options.* Trumbull: Weatherhill.

we will have to act as one. If we are going to fight the spread of HIV/AIDS around the globe we have to work as one. If we are going to provide clean running water to underdeveloped countries we will have to pull our resources together as one. We cannot fool ourselves to think that we can accomplish anything by ourselves. We cannot, for one minute, think that we have enough stamina or resources to accomplish these great tasks on our own. Imagine what more could be accomplished if we all pulled our resources and ideas together.

"We develop our full humanity by fulfilling our needs and the needs of others, Confucius declares."[84] Can we genuinely make the statement that we are living up to our fullest potential when we do not expand ourselves for the wellbeing of others? You cannot be fully human, in my opinion, until you have helped someone else to live. Until you have helped supply the needs of someone other than yourself you have no idea what grace has been bestowed upon you. Until you look into the eyes of a person living on the streets as they gleam for one pair of socks, you will never understand how blessed you are. Until you see the child death rate dropping in Ghana because there is no contaminated water, will you appreciate the Dasani™ water you are fortunate to have. It is not until you deliver the box of prepackaged meals to the elderly in your community do you appreciate the fact that your grandmother still cooks for you. If a Christian has a true desire to live for Christ they can do such by connecting to the needs of others. I have come in contact with countless volunteers who have come to the realization that serving may deplete you physically, but it rejuvenates you spiritually. When you can see the work of God being done through you it gives a person a new sense of purpose and direction.

However, we will never reach the place of personal enlightenment if we are unwilling to answer to what is happening around us. If we were to analyze our current

---

[84] Carter, Lawrence Edward, George David Miller, and Neelakanta Radhakrishnan. 2001. *Global Ethical Options*. Trumbull: Weatherhill.

society could we truly say that we have acted on the social, ethical and humanitarian injustices that are still prevalent? As we look across mainstream media, and social media, we can see exactly what the issues are and where they are most prevalent. We are able to see, first hand, communities that need support and restoration. The breaking news on our television and syndicated radio stations are often connected to a wrong doing or social injustice. Yet we continue to flip through the channels of acceptance in hopes there will be a new story tomorrow. We continue to sit on our couches, in front of our computer screens, and glued to our smart devices, with no intent to move in the direction of change and reconciliation. An important element of cooperation is responsiveness.

According to Dean Carter, "Cooperation with others depends upon embracing them and respecting their differences."[85] We must place our personal agendas and promotions to the side in an effort to address the root issues that plague our communities. We must learn how to take the side of truth and justice and not stand on the side of the victims or the oppressors. We must embrace the feelings of all with a heart of understanding, compassion, sympathy and empathy. There must be a point in history where we stop advocating and start acting. We must approach these climates in the world with the consciousness to uphold the autonomous value of others.

This is what helps define Christians as people of virtue. The word virtue has a lot of meaning, and means many different things to various people, but can be a trait or disposition of character that leads to good behavior. One example is that someone with virtue displays wisdom, courage, kindness, good manners, courtesy, modesty, generosity, and self-control in their life. They treat others fairly and esteem others highly and value the sanctity of life. They treat others better than they are

---

[85] Carter, Lawrence Edward, George David Miller, and Neelakanta Radhakrishnan. 2001. *Global Ethical Options*. Trumbull: Weatherhill.

treated. Someone who has virtue has good, moral ethics and makes biblical choices in life. We must understand that as Christians it is our choice to act virtuously and that becoming a Christian does not make us automatically virtuous. According to Aristotle we must consider the execution of our virtues as a foundation for humanitarian giving and community development. He says, "Next we must consider what virtue is. Since things that are found in the soul are of three kinds- passions, faculties, states of character, virtue must be one of these."[86] The virtues outlined in the biblical text should also be connected to our passions, abilities and character. While Aristotle suggests that our virtues must be connected to one of the aforementioned, I believe that the virtues of God can be connected to all of the above.

It takes a conscious effort to make these connections and build these relationships. As Aristotle states, this must take root at the level of the soul. Our actions must come from a place called the heart. But more importantly our hearts ought to be connected to the heart of God.

Aristotle concludes that, "Virtue, then, is a state of character concerned with choice, lying in a mean, i.e. the mean relative to us, this being determined by a rational principle, and by that principle by which the man of practical wisdom would determine it."[87] We must be courageous enough to choose to do virtuous acts. We must choose to help the marginalized and the oppressed. We must choose to help those who are unable to help themselves. We must choose to show grace on those who have been beat up by the systems of society. We have the option to choose right action over comfortability. To defeat this comfortability we ought to be willing to tie ourselves to the problems of the world until they are resolved. Virtue for the sake of self-advancement and personal gain should be thrown out the window. Virtue for the

---

[86] Aristotle. 1997. *Nichomachean Ethics*. London: Wordsworth.

[87] Aristotle. 1997. *Nichomachean Ethics*. London: Wordsworth.

sake of a better world, a stronger sense of community and a quest for the manifestation of God's love here on earth should be adopted. We should be determined to prove God in the eyes of those who don't believe that God's presence is in common welfare of the world around us. God is present in the works of humanity. But God's presence can only be experienced if we offer ourselves as agents for Him to work through.

THE COST OF SERVICE FOR THE CHRISTIAN BELIEVER
It will cost you something personally to provide liberty and freedom for another.

It is unfortunate to say many modern millennial Christians will never get to this point of personal sacrifice. Many modern millennials have become extremely selfish and self-centered. No longer do we observe youth and young adults as excited as they were to serve in years past. We can see many millennials adopting a non-religious model of spirituality. Most millennial Christians have no idea they are connected to things that are not "Christian". We have failed to ingrain in their minds their connection with the world around them. We have pushed the separation of the sacred and the secular. As a result the modern millennial Christian stands in confusion as to how they should be in the church versus how they are challenged to be in the community. There is a lie that has been told to the world: **the sacred and the secular are separate.** As I have come to learn over time, this is a falsehood. God is in all things. I believe the moment modern millennial Christians see they are connected with the marginalized and the oppressed is the moment they will see the importance of their role in service.

We do not become virtuous except by acting virtuously. We cannot prove ourselves as Christians until we do things that are Christ like. We will not be respected in the community until we begin doing community work. We will not see peace, grace and love exhibited in the world until we choose to be those things in our personal environment. Practice makes perfect. As a result, what we desire to see perfected in life and our communities must be practiced in our everyday walk. As Aristotle asserts, we can only become courageous by acting courageously.[88] There are many virtues that Jesus challenges us to perform, and make reality, in our daily walk. Some are deemed easier than others but to say they least they all require a certain level of diligence and

---

[88] Aristotle. 1997. *Nichomachean Ethics.* London: Wordsworth.

commitment. We cannot continue to call ourselves something that we are unwilling to act upon if called out.

It is untrue to say the person living with HIV, the woman who is caught in the sex trafficking business and the town lacking clean running water have no connection to the Christian faith. As I near the close of this text I want to make it clear that we are all connected to one another. The Christian is connected to the atheist. The single parent is connected to the double parent household. The person who experiences homelessness is connected to the person who owns multiple real estate properties. The person living with perfect health is connected to the person living with HIV. The unemployed is connected to the business owner. The religious person is connected to the spiritual person. The commonality is that these are the situations we are called to 'go' and address. We have been challenged to build the bridges that separate these communities of people. We have been challenged to hold the hands of those who have been let go by others. The truth is these things are a part of our human existence, which can't be separated from our Christian existence. Whether we experience one, or observe the other, we are simultaneously experiencing them in the same consciousness. I blame the colonization era for this perpetuation of lies. This era of time initiated the "let US go help THEM" mentality. We must be noble enough to trumpet the truth that there is no them or us and that to help one is to help all; including the helper.

We must be true and loyal to the message Christ gave us generations ago. We cannot grown weary in our efforts to create the world Christ intended for us to occupy. We cannot give up on the hope that Jesus gave us when He left us His spirit as a reminder of His presence here on earth:

> [15]"If you love me, obey my commandments. [16]And I will ask the Father, and he will give you another Advocate, who will never leave you. [17]He is the Holy Spirit, who leads into all truth. The world

cannot receive him, because it isn't looking for him and doesn't recognize him. But you know him, because he lives with you now and later will be in you. ¹⁸No, I will not abandon you as orphans—I will come to you. ¹⁹Soon the world will no longer see me, but you will see me. Since I live, you also will live. ²⁰When I am raised to life again, you will know that I am in my Father, and you are in me, and I am in you. ²¹Those who accept my commandments and obey them are the ones who love me. And because they love me, my Father will love them. And I will love them and reveal myself to each of them." (John 14:15-21)

Loyalty is devotion to a cause over a long period of time, according to Josiah Royce and John Dewey. The loyal person actively supports causes. A person demonstrates loyalty to the cause of ending world hunger by a long and sustained commitment to it and acting to support it. According to this view, loyalty to the community is a long-term or even life-long project.[89] We are still fighting social, oppressive, marginalized and economic factors that were present in the Old Testament. Does this mean that these issues will never be resolved? No. What this means is that these issues will stay with us as a reminder of the work we need to do for Christ, and with Christ. Our quest to make the world a better place is continuous because the world always has the potential to become a better world. We cannot do what we do for humanity to see an end result. Instead we should act as human change agents because we feel as though it is our responsibility to do so regardless of the ultimate outcome.

While Jesus, King and Ghandi have transitioned into another consciousness of life, there are present day champions who still carry the torch for humanitarian service and responsibility. Daisaku Ikeda is a Buddhist philosopher, educator, author, and anti-nuclear activist who presently serves as the third president of the Soka Gakkai, which is the largest of Japan's new religious movements. I learned much

---

[89] Royce, Josiah. 1995. *The Phiilosophy of Loyalty*. Nashville: Vanderbilt University Press.

about his views and philosophies while I was studying at Morehouse College. While he practices the ancient near eastern religion of Buddhism I do believe the underline message in his principles are supported by the biblical text. Ikeda speaks in his lecture at Columbia University June 13, 1996 that the essential elements of Global Citizenship are: 1. The wisdom to perceive the interconnectedness of all life and living, 2. The courage not to fear or deny difference: but to respect and strive to understand people of different cultures, and to grow from encounters with them, and 3. The compassion to maintain an imaginative empathy that reaches beyond one's immediate surroundings and extends to those sufferings in distant places.[90] What is consistent in his summation, as well as the model of Christ, is that compassion for the world will solve the disparities of humanity. We must be reminded of the power of love that is illustrated in the scriptures:

> [1]If I could speak all the languages of earth and of angels, but didn't love others, I would only be a noisy gong or a clanging cymbal. [2]If I had the gift of prophecy, and if I understood all of God's secret plans and possessed all knowledge, and if I had such faith that I could move mountains, but didn't love others, I would be nothing. [3]If I gave everything I have to the poor and even sacrificed my body, I could boast about it; but if I didn't love others, I would have gained nothing. [4]Love is patient and kind. Love is not jealous or boastful or proud [5]or rude. It does not demand its own way. It is not irritable, and it keeps no record of being wronged. [6]It does not rejoice about injustice but rejoices whenever the truth wins out. [7]Love never gives up, never loses faith, is always hopeful, and endures through every circumstance. [8]Prophecy and speaking in unknown languages and special knowledge will become useless. But love will last forever! [9]Now our knowledge is partial and incomplete, and even the gift of prophecy reveals only part of the whole picture! [10]But when the time of perfection comes, these partial things will become useless. [11]When I was a child, I spoke and thought and reasoned as a child. But when I grew up, I put away childish things. [12]Now we see things imperfectly, like puzzling reflections in a mirror, but then we will see everything with perfect clarity. All that I know now is partial and

---

[90] Carter, Lawrence Edward, George David Miller, and Neelakanta Radhakrishnan. 2001. *Global Ethical Options*. Trumbull: Weatherhill.

incomplete, but then I will know everything completely, just as God now knows me completely. ¹³Three things will last forever—faith, hope, and love—and the greatest of these is love. (1 Corinthians 13)

We must begin to educate ourselves as well as future generations of the power that couples with love and how that power has the potential to transform communities. True love has never started wars. True love has never perpetuated world hunger or poverty. True love has never left the marginalized outside of the margins. True love has never refused a person the experience of a happy life at the expense of someone else's comfortability. True love has never made a person to feel as though they are less than the other. In the same regard, genuine Christians have never made the community feel isolated from the unconditional love of God. Aristotle says, "Hence we ought to have been brought up in a particular way from out very youth, as Plato says, so as both to delight in and to be pained by the things that we ought; for this is the right education."[91] Likewise, our children and our children's children should be taught in such a way where they understand that the solution to a world filled with hatred, bigotry, genocide, oppression, homicide, brutality, poverty, economic despair and social disparities will be rooted in compassion, consideration, thoughtfulness, kindness, benevolence, responsiveness and empathy.

Yet again, we must chose to be a part of this world transformation. The list above is very extensive yet it does not touch the tip of the ice burg to what needs to be displayed in our communities. There are countless other traits I believe we should be on the lookout for. To create each of these in our personal reality may appear as a tall mountain to climb. Yet, with careful consideration, and courageous execution, the above mentioned can be mastered by any person who is willing to travel the road of Christ consciousness and enlightenment. We will discuss these concepts in more detail later in the text. However, at the end of the day, what we need to be aiming

---

[91] Aristotle. 1997. *Nichomachean Ethics.* London: Wordsworth.

towards is developing a resilience to the uphill battle of service. As it has demonstrated itself in history that it will not be an easy task to reconcile the world back to God and humanitarian responsibility; but it is our ordained task and we will be held accountable by God for its success. Aristotle says, "It is difficult sometimes to determine what should be chosen and at what cost, and what should be endured in return for what gain, and yet more difficult to abide by your decisions."[92] We can choose to be the church goers or we can chose to be Christians. We can choose to be preachers or we can choose to be the trombones who sound the clarion call for change. We can choose to be observers of change or we can become active participants in that change. We can throw our resources at building projects and self-serving ministry agendas or we can gather our possessions to help communities who are without. Either way we will choose to stand on the side of the change agents or the comfortable Christians.

With the biblical roadmap that is accessible to us, we should utilize the bible and other religious resources as our GPS system towards humanitarian change. We have everything we need in the word of God. We have the greatest energy source backing our every move. The bible provides us with a time tested method of execution that can catapult us into a renewed sense of consciousness. Kouzes and Posner describe how we as Christians should be leading the current community in their book *The Leadership Challenge*. They say that leaders are pioneers- people who are willing to step out into the unknown. They are people who are willing to take risks, to innovate and experiment in order to find new and better ways of doing things.[93] While much of the world has been discovered, there is still the potential for pioneers to be birthed. In an effort to make the world a more Christ centered place we must be willing to take risks. True Christians will be open to all of the possibilities and the risks associated with them. However, with those risks, innovation and improvement is

---

[92] Aristotle. 1997. *Nichomachean Ethics.* London: Wordsworth.

[93] Kouzes, James M., and Barry Z. Posner. 1994. *The Leadership Challenge.* New York: Warner Books.

birthed. The moment we take the risks is the moment we secure a form of spiritual, and empirical, return. We will not improve the face of the globe unless we are courageous enough to take pioneering possibilities. We should never cease in our quest to improve the ways we can make civilization a better place.

Each day I seek to perform something at The Worship Center that is out of the norm, I have to take into account the risks associated with it. It is only human for me to think about what others say and how they perceive our ministry actions. There are countless opportunities where I question the voice of God because of the risks, I know, that are associated with its execution. When we set out to take on our first international missions project to build a clean water system in the Dominican Republic, at 8 months old, there was a major risk associated with our ability to produce what God had spoken to me. We did not have the positive cash flow to make it happen. We did not have the weekly attendance that I thought we needed to energize this project. We were just breaking even with our present operational expenses. How in the world could we produce an international project that would literally cost us thousands of dollars and countless man hours to produce? At the end of our campaign God answered the call! To this day I think back and ask myself the question, "What if I didn't take the risk to build a clean water system in the Dominican Republic?"

God is looking for a generation of change agents who are willing to take risks while placing their complete confidence in the abilities of God. Max DePree reminds us that "by avoiding risk we really risk what's most important in life-reaching toward growth, our potential, and a true contribution to a common goal. Wherever or however we serve, we can't avoid the central conundrum of risk: to risk nothing is perhaps the greatest risk of all."[94]

---

[94] DePree, Max. 1997. *Leading without Power*. San Francisco: Jossey-Bass.

As a leader I have learned that the greater the risk the larger the reward. What I have learned as a religious leader is that the greater the risk the larger our God becomes to the world. As we look back on history at the countless risk takers who championed change in their communities, we can observe that their greatest accomplishments came when they placed their complete confidence in God. What we can learn from those who came before us is that our ability to create sustainable change is founded in our courageousness to jump off the cliff while others remain on the ground. As Gene Wilkes points out in *Jesus on Leadership: Discovering the Secrets of Servant Leadership from the Life of Christ*, "A leader is a pioneer because she goes to the edge of a current reality and takes the next step. Upon seeing the new reality, she invites others to join her on the edge. Not everyone is drawn to the edge, but most people admire those who stand out.[95]" What steps are we willing to take to ensure that humanity experiences the love of God? While countless people have tapped out in the race towards change, we should continue to run with the hope that our perseverance will produce something mighty. We ought to challenge others to join us in this race, and to make a stand for social change. If the church, and Christianity, seek to regain their relevancy in the community, and the world at large, it must do something that will spawn admiration and awe from its onlookers.

To move to the front line as an advocate for change and social responsibility also means to place one's self at the front line of ridicule and attacks. To make the attempt to change the mindset and consciousness of others is an extremely dangerous tasks. To suggest what someone ought to do infringes, and implies that what they are currently doing is incorrect or in need of improvement. This can cause a person to become defensive regarding their current work or service. But as Doug Murren, in his book *Leadershift*, states, "All paradigm pioneers have a different spirit from the naysayers about them. They have the ability to see a new thing, to perceive a bright

---

[95] Wilkes, C. Gene. 1998. *Jesus on Leadership: Discovering the Secrets of Servant Leadership from the Life of Christ.* Wheaton: Tyndale House Publishers.

future, to tap into the power of God."[96] In other words we cannot be concerned about what others are saying as long as we hold on to the truth of what God says about us. We must have a commitment to see the world for the potential it has and hope for that future to manifest itself. When we become weak and worrisome we should tap into the strength of our creator, champion and charge giver. We cannot fool ourselves to think that the road to re-establishing church and Christian relevancy in the community will be easy. However, someone must be courageous enough to run the race.

As we push in the direction of change, we can note that our faith and trust in God will be the driving force that keeps us going. We must place our full dependency on God as the ultimate change maker. True change agents understand their role as an extension of divine energy. As that extension they are also made aware of the risks associated with declaring work, and actions, on behalf of God. Wilkes states that, "When we trust that God is in control of our life, we can take big risks. We can relinquish impressive positions. We can act like true servants without being insecure or defensive."[97] We should be unafraid to dream and do big for humanity when we know that God's power and anointing is over our actions. God's word promises that we will not be ashamed or embarrassed for our obedience. God's word further lets us know that His reputation is on the line with our actions. For us to fail could imply that God is a liar, or that our challenge for change was not divinely ordered. But when we relinquish self, and place the needs of others before our own, God becomes glorified in our actions. True millennial Christians have no concern for sitting at the head table when a curbside meal with the marginalized would make the heart of God flutter.

---

[96] Murren, Doug. 1994. *Leadershift*. Ventura: Regal.

[97] Wilkes, C. Gene. 1998. *Jesus on Leadership: Discovering the Secrets of Servant Leadership from the Life of Christ*. Wheaton: Tyndale House Publishers.

However, as I have learned over the course of my service career, God will exalt those who humble themselves. God will open doors you never requested to be opened. God will provide resources and favor on projects you anticipated struggle. However, what the millennial should understand is that these pleasures are unwarranted, regardless of what we do or how often we serve. Therefore one cannot forget the source of all grace and love. We cannot overlook the truth that our accomplishments are only made possible through the power of God. As Wilkes continues, "You did not earn your place at the head table. God chose you for that place. Your fear to risk that place for the mission of God points to your lack of trust in the God who got you there."[98] God has strategically positioned us in specific environments to serve specific communities of people. You may question why you are in a specific city. You may wonder why you are drawn to a certain marginalized group of people. You may have questioned why you feel a certain level of compassion towards a definite cause. What you have to remember is that you were placed on this planet for a purpose. What we also must adopt is that our purpose is connected to the well-being of another.

There are many populations of people, some outlined in this text, who feel as though the church has forgotten about them. There are people who feel as though the modern Christian has left them alone in the world with no sense of hope or love. As we look out into the condition of mankind we cannot overlook the feelings held by the oppressed and the marginalized. We must take into consideration the depression, stress, fear, hopelessness and loneliness experienced by these communities of people. As Henri Nouwen states, "When we look into the eyes of young people, we can catch a glimpse of at least a shadow of their lonely world."[99] If

---

[98] Wilkes, C. Gene. 1998. *Jesus on Leadership: Discovering the Secrets of Servant Leadership from the Life of Christ.* Wheaton: Tyndale House Publishers.

[99] Nouwen, Henri J. M. 1972. *The Wounded Healer: Ministry in Contemporary Society.* New York: Doubleday Religion.

we are going to reach the present generation, and future generation, of believers and non-believers, we will have to exercise empathy for the present state of their world. The spirit of understanding marries well with the spirit of compassion. We may not be able to fully understand the condition or circumstances of our brothers and sisters. However, we can be courageous enough to enter into the darkness with them in order to help bring them to the light. As a matter of fact, our goal may not always be to bring them into the light but rather to carry our light to them.

RE-ESTABLISHING A SENSE OF COMMUNITY: THE "US" FACTOR

Instead, the mindset of the modern millennial Christian should be
"Let US help and Care for US"!

The bible supports the consciousness I like to call **'the other as me'**. The scriptures tell us, *"In your relationships with one another, have the same mindset as Christ Jesus: Who, being in very nature God, did not consider equality with God something to be used to his own advantage; rather, he made himself nothing by taking the very nature of a servant, being made in human likeness." Philippians 2:5-7 NIV* We have to be willing to tap into the mentality of Jesus. If we are going to regain relevancy in the community we must begin to think like Jesus. There has to be a willingness to do, and take the risks Jesus did while he was present here on earth. If Jesus pledged to the model of servanthood then so should we. The embodiment of God in human form was the ultimate display of God connecting with humanity. Jesus coming to this reality we call earth was God's way of reconnecting to His creations. Jesus coming to earth was more than just about salvation, it was about making the world aware of its responsibility to the other.

In the same way, we must learn to embody the plight of the marginalized as our own. Responsibility and accountability will be our first and last name when we get to heaven. We cannot wait until the misfortune hits home until when we all share this geographic body called earth. The modern millennial cannot wait until issues reach our back yard to make the decision to act. We cannot wear, with pride, our Christian hats and t-shirts when there are still men, women and children who heads and bodies are cold from their winters of sleeping on the streets. The modern millennial Christian should not be comfortable while countless persons experience uncomfortability as a way of life. We can't keep pushing our bible teachings on 'Jesus as the living water' when there are still countries that don't have access to uncontaminated running water. We cannot proclaim the truth that God is a healer when we have deemed HIV/AIDS as incurable. We cannot continue to preach that

Jesus purchased our salvation if we are unwilling to fight for those who are purchased for sexual favors. If God can come to earth in human likeness, True Christians can present themselves in the world as equal and not superior. If Gods desire was to feel humanity, a True Christians desire should be to feel the pains of the oppressed, downtrodden and marginalized.

If Jesus can humble himself to think of himself on the same level as humanity, then certainly we can as True Christians. When a person accepts Christ they should also accept and adopt the mindset, and consciousness, of Christ. The whole belief in Jesus is centered on the idea that God doesn't mind associating God's self with the totality of humankind. What can be noted throughout the biblical text is that God feels, experiences and has compassion in the same way humanity does. The issue found with most traditional Christians is they believe their Christian association separates them from the rest of humanity. They believe that to have the title of Christian places them in an elite, and separate, group of people. This could not be far from the truth that Christ intended for His generation, and the generations to follow. The term "Christian" should actually spawn the opposite consciousness.

Liberation theologian Gustavo Gutierrez reminds us "To know Yahweh, which in biblical language is equivalent to saying to love Yahweh, is to establish just relationships among persons, it is to recognize the rights of the poor. The God of biblical revelation is known through interhuman justice. When justice does not exist, God is not known, God is absent.[100] To know God is to love God. To know humanity is to develop compassion for humanity. To know the oppressed is to engage with the oppressed. To understand the marginalized is to dialogue with the marginalized. In order to know anything, a person must be willing to enter into some type of relationship with that thing. Therefore, the God we see acting in the biblical text, as

---

[100] Gutierrez, Gustavo. 1998. *Liberation Theology and the Future of the Poor.* Minneapolis: Fortress Press.

well as the God we see in operation today, is known by His relationship with the world. I agree with Gutierrez in that God's presence will consciously remain with us when we connect our Christian actions to the work of humanity and the betterment of the world. As I have stated in the onset of this text, I believe that people have lost sight of the presence of God in the world because they do not see the extensions of God in operation throughout the world.

If the church, and Christianity, is going to become relevant in today's world it is going to take a redefining moment. It must involve the church and Christianity redefining itself and its involvement in the workings of the world. While Christianity is still one of the leading religions in the world it does not mean that the practices and dogma are automatically correct. I believe that people assume that as one of the dominant religions, Christianity represents a group of people who have the right answer for all things. While the standards of God's word offer us a blueprint for moral and ethical living, I believe that the faith at large needs to take an inward look as to how we execute the greatest commandments of Christ himself.

According to psychoanalyst Jacques Lacan, those from the dominant culture look into the mirror and recognize themselves as superior through the distancing process of negative self-definition: "I am what I am not." The subject "I" is defined by contrasting it with the Objects residing on the margins. In the formation of the "I" out of the difference from the "them," there exist established power relations that give meaning to those differences.[101] To be a Christian does not separate you from being human, or from showing compassion towards the injustices and oppressive states of humanity. We are not Christian because we are not experiencing homelessness. We are not Christian because we have clean running water in our communities. We are not Christian because we are not connected to human sex

---

[101] Lacan, Jacques. 1977. *Ecrits: A Selection.* Trans. Alan Sheridan. New York: W. W. Norton.

trafficking. We are not Christian because we are not connected to or associated with substance abuse and domestic violence. We are Christians because of the compassion and relationships we have with these communities.

What Christians can teach the world is that we are all connected as God's children. What we can learn from the biblical text is that the prostitute is no different from the magistrate in God's eyes. What we can observe is that the tax collector is no less than the priest. Today we can conclude that the exotic dancer is no different from the politician. We can clearly see that the CEOs of the world are no different than our Pastors. We are all human and we all have the right to experience humanity in a compassionate way. We are all connected because, according to Christian belief, we all share a lineage that dates back to Adam and Eve. Therefore, "We must treat people as equals with openness and caring, we enter into what Martin Buber calls an "I-Thou" relationship. The absence of those qualities reduces the relationship to an "I-It" relationship. Threatening another as "It" reduces the relationship to an "I-It" relationship."[102] If we are going to be strong leaders in the community we cannot base our relationships with others based on their conditions in societies. It is not what people are, or what they have done, our challenge is to connect with who they are and who they have the potential to be. From the person experiencing homelessness to the person living with HIV. From the single parent, to the individual who has been caught up in the sex trade industry. From the person who cannot afford a collegiate education, to the person who does not have the resources to produce clean running water; we are all a family who share the common goal to experience life to its fullest potential.

The world does not need more religious practitioners. The world does not need more people coming together to worship in churches on Sunday morning. The

---

[102] Buber, Martin. 1970. *I and Thou.* New York: Klaus Reprint.

world does not need any more denominational conventions and conferences. The world does not need any more bible studies or small groups. What the world needs is more people who actually practice their faith. What the world needs is more people who are willing to come together for community work instead of worship alone. What the world needs is a community of people who will study culture and policies in order to improve the way of living and the state of humanity. Elisabeth Kubler-Ross says that "The world is in desperate need of loving people who can cooperate and care for others: its not what others offer, but what we can offer others."[103] Where are the lovers of the world? Where are the people who show compassion on the oppressed and the marginalized? Where are those who are willing to work on right side of the aisle and the left side of the aisle? Where are the people who are willing to work with the resource holders and those who don't have? We should know by now that it is not about what our communities can do for the church and the Christian community, but what the body of Christ at large can do for the community.

Dr. Martin Luther King says that there must be a recognition of the sacredness of human personality. Deeply rooted in our political and religious heritage is the conviction that every man is an heir to a legacy of dignity and worth.[104] If the push towards an "us" is the primary focus of modern millennial Christians, then what modern millennial Christians must hold as valuable is the poise and value of all people. The truth that God made each of us autonomous to one another is a divine point of enlightenment within itself. The notion that none of us are exactly alike, yet all interconnected by divine energy, is to be commended by our Creator. God knew what God was doing when God created each of us. God knew what God was doing what God placed us in the specific environments, and communities, we find ourselves

---

[103] Carter, Lawrence Edward, George David Miller, and Neelakanta Radhakrishnan. 2001. *Global Ethical Options*. Trumbull: Weatherhill.

[104] Carter, Lawrence Edward, George David Miller, and Neelakanta Radhakrishnan. 2001. *Global Ethical Options*. Trumbull: Weatherhill.

frequenting. If we are going to be fully effective in our quest to manifest God's presence here on earth we must be courageous enough to see what others can't, or are unwilling to, see in the marginalized and the oppressed communities of the world. Dignity and worth should be at the pupil of our focus as we look out into the world.

The great leader Daisaku Ikeda spoke in his speech on January 31, 1993 the words of Nichiren Daishonin as he writes, "If you light a lantern for another, it will also brighten your own way." Please be confident that the higher you burn the flame of altruistic action, the more its light will suffuse your life with happiness. Those who possess an altruistic spirit are the happiest people of all.[105] When we learn to give to others we will soon discover that we are also giving to ourselves. When we learn to embrace the oppressed and marginalized communities we will soon notice that we are loving on our own. The more we help others who are indirectly connected to us the more we are helping the groups, and communities of people who are directly connected to us. To bring someone out of darkness and into the light, would require us, also, going down the dark path and utilizing that same light to guide us back to community change and personal enlightenment. People who are altruistic, unselfish, humane, philanthropic, noble, and self-sacrificing in their actions find the greatest joys in life.

Another path to knowing, and this personal model of enlightenment has been suggested by Ellen Berscheid. She suggests as a point of departure, "interpersonal knowing" which includes both social intelligence (knowing other people and oneself) and social competence (the ability to produce the desired responses in interaction with others).[106] If the church and the Christianity are going to regain relevancy in modern

---

[105] Carter, Lawrence Edward, George David Miller, and Neelakanta Radhakrishnan. 2001. *Global Ethical Options*. Trumbull: Weatherhill.

[106] Berscheid, Ellen. n.d. "Interpersonal Modes of Knowing." In *Learning and Teaching the Ways of Knowing*, by Eisner, 60-76.

culture they must stay up to date on the current happenings of society. These sacred communities of people must stay abreast on the up-to-date issues and problems that our communities faces. They must be willing to keep their ears on the lips of God as well as the cries of the people. At the same rate they cannot continue to separate what they hear as something that is other than them. What we must understand is that to know about one another is to also know about one's self. As we engage with these communities we will soon discover our own fears, guilt, inadequacies, and uncomfortabilities. We will also recognize is our personal abilities to make impactful community change. We will discover that our passions are truly connected to our purpose and that our calling in life is to create better communities and not separate sects of religious, or spiritual, practitioners.

THE BRAND OF CHRISTIANITY IN THE EYES OF HUMANITY

The association of the word "Christian" in the community should connect the carrier of the brand (Christianity) with the responsibility, and personal accountability, of connecting others with humanity as self.

Over the course of history, Christianity has become a religious brand. There are specific characteristics that help others identify the Christian faith. There are a few specific things that Christians do that would separate them from other religions. I could exhaust an extensive list, but my concern regarding the brand of Christianity is that the faith has become less known for its works in the community over the years. As I have stated before, there was a time in history when people knew you were a Christian because of the service you put forth in the world. I believe this pivotal element to the brand of Christianity needs to be brought to the forefront of our attention today. Jesus himself began to engrain this message of service into his followers. What I believe Jesus was trying to turn our ears to was the very specific message of altruism. If we were to look at the teachings of Jesus we would be able to see much of what he taught had nothing to do with the happenings located in the four walls of church. Rather, Jesus wanted to teach people how to be people.

Jesus taught how people should be willing to give their lives for the betterment of others. He taught people that the work of God is in the streets. He taught that worship has its place, however we cannot forget about the work God placed us on this planet to do. One particular scripture that comes to mind is found in the gospel of Mark. The text says, *"Sitting down, Jesus called the Twelve and said, 'Anyone who wants to be first must be the very last, and the servant of all." Mark 9:35 NIV* In this statement, Jesus was giving us the key to success and relevancy: service. Notice how Jesus does not mention service to a specific community of people, but rather awakens the consciousness of the disciples to know that humanity at large is in need of the love of Christ. He showed us how to move to the top of the class, and to the head of the table, with his wise words. This principle proves to be very evident in today's culture as well. Think of some of the most successful persons in the world. Then consider how much of their accomplishments are connected to their service and philanthropic efforts. Think about the large foundations they fund, give to, and have created. The reality is that God blesses those who choose to bless others. Pastors and religious leaders scratch their heads trying to figure out why church seats are empty. I would venture to say the church has not reached, or connected with, the community to fill those seats.

Jesus articulates to us to be people of provision. The words of Christ have always encouraged us with the truth that God will supply every resource we need to be successful and influential. Jesus' message pushes us to the point where we have to reconsider what our true purpose is as human, and not necessarily as an orthodox Christian. Jesus declares to literally place ourselves at the back of the line and to contemplate placing the needs of others ahead of our own. This particular scripture also gives the modern millennial Christians the assignment to care for all! While we, as individuals, can't touch every aspect of humanity we should be willing to touch the broad base of the world at the level that leaves no one excluded. We can't fix all the problems of the world, but our presence can be felt in the community as people who support the quest for solutions.

The actuality is we all have been given liberty and freedom in life. We all can attest to the point that we have come from a place of oppression. While some may not have had the situations of another, it is a true statement that no one starts at the top. Each of us, through the grace and mercy of God, have risen to the levels we find ourselves today. But how many of us have forgotten to consider those whose journey out of oppression is much more of a challenge than our own? Despite the fact I lived in a state of homelessness for almost a year, the process it took for me to get back on my feet was much shorter than those I come in contact with each week on the streets of Atlanta. I have been arrested for a felony, however my process of going through the judicial system was much quicker than others. My point is we have all been in the darkness of life and made our way to the light. For those who are still experiencing their process, we must be patient, and supportive, as they complete their journey.

We should be willing to help others find the same liberty and freedom we have been graced. We should live our lives in such a way where we don't get too relaxed with our fortune to the point we forget about the misfortunes of others. The scriptures even tell us, *"You, my brothers and sisters, were called to be free. But do not use your freedom to indulge the flesh; rather, serve one another humbly in love"* Galatians 5:13 NIV. There should be a trickle of God's love that flows from our lives to the lives of others. The grace God bestows upon us should be extended to those living in oppressive situations. The hope we have discovered in the word of God should be echoed in our daily conversations with those who have lost hope in their realities. True Christians know they have been given their freedom for the purpose of helping others. Comfortable Christians are those who see their liberty as a blessing, but have turned a blind eye to the oppression of others.

The free and the oppressed have much in common. A person may not think it, but those who are on the top rings of life have much in common with those we view as being on the bottom of the ladder. Nevertheless, the person who experiences freedom may never admit this truth until they are willing to relate and touch the needs of the oppressed. Whenever people come out to feed the homeless with The Worship Center, there is this continued consciousness and observation made by all our volunteers; the people in the line receiving food look no different from those in the line giving the meals.

Modern Christians should be comfortable with the statement that there is nothing that separates the Jew from the Gentile, the homeless person from the mansion owner, the single mother from the married with child woman, the person living with HIV from the person in perfect health. The bible paints for us the picture for what true community should look like: *"Everyone was filled with awe at the many wonders and signs performed by the apostles. All the believers were together and had everything in common. They sold property and possessions to give to anyone who had need"* Acts 2:43-45 NIV Our commonality is that we are all human beings experiencing this consciousness called life on this environment called earth.

Let's be genuine, most Christians have more than enough to take care of what they need in life. True Christians understand their overflow should be used in order to help the poor and the oppressed. Miguel De La Torre supports my argument when he writes, "It is not what is said that bears witness to the good news of the resurrection, but what is done to those still trapped in the forces of death."[107] Christians can preach the message that Jesus was raised from the dead until they are blue in the face. Nevertheless, until they can rightfully articulate why He was resurrected, the world will never understand that this action was connect to ultimate sacrifice and love for another.

The modern church cannot continue to preach a prosperity gospel based on the tangible blessings of God without bringing to the consciousness of others that all of God's blessings are not empirical. There should be a willingness, and a revolution, that should not separate God from things and actions but rather paints God in the light of being the ultimate love source. The modern Christian should not be lost in what God can do for them. We should not be lost in the works of the church that we forget the works of the world. We cannot become lost in our denominations and ordinances that we lose focus of the church universal. The modern Christian has to make the conscious decision to become lost in the assignment to serve humanity and

---

[107] Torre, Miguel A De La. 2004. *Doing Christian Ethics from the Margins.* Maryknoll: Orbis Books.

others. As Dean Lawrence Carter states, "When we commune with the highest, strive for the best, and lose ourselves in others, we rise above the material possessions of life and discover a peace that is beyond our understanding."[108] Fellowship with God should trump our fellowship with self-serving activities. Our quest to be the best, and to create the best in the world around us, should be observed in our everyday stride. When we become lost in serving others, it is at that core where we circle back and find our greatest connection to God. It is at that point of connecting back to God and humanity that we experience a euphoric peace and assurance that God's love is still present in the world.

There is a circle of life, and a system for service, that I believe will offer us solutions as well as place us on the right track back to relevancy and divine results. We must trust our **intuition.** Our instinct and sensitivity towards the issues of the world will always play a role in our willingness to move, or our reluctance to act. As you read about the issues discussed in the forefront of this text there was an instinctive response you felt. Maybe it was, "We should do something about this", or "That's not fair", or "I did not know these conditions were this bad". Either way, when we are presented with these woes in our everyday life there is an instinctive response. When you see the person on the corner with the "will work for food" sign. When you watch the media and see terroristic acts taking place locally and internationally. When you watch that commercial soliciting financial support for a country living in poverty.

That sensitivity and tug on our hearts should cause us to act. Even if not in that moment we should trust our gut with the underline instinct that something needs to be done. Needless to say, before we implement our strategies and action plans we must be **rational.** There are countless critiques I can give regarding the execution of some social, political, economic and environmental agendas for change. However, my

---

[108] Carter, Lawrence Edward, George David Miller, and Neelakanta Radhakrishnan. 2001. *Global Ethical Options*. Trumbull: Weatherhill.

biggest analysis is that there are groups of people who mean well, but don't always think through their implementation. As a result, very few end goals are accomplished or very little progress is made towards change. The work we do as Christians should make sense. The ministries and projects we endorse and create should be well thought out before executed.

Once this has been taken into account we must be **caring** while we push forward for change and transformation. Evil cannot be fought with evil. In the same regard we cannot have our actions breed more hatred and separation. Love and compassion should be evident in whatever we choose to do. Care and consideration for the wellbeing and feelings of others ought to be our primary concern. Finally, we must **rely totally on the written and audible word of God** in our lives. As Christians, we should consult the religious text we call the Bible while keeping our spiritual ears open for what God wants to communicate to us today. I personally have adopted this model as an extension of Dean Lawrence Carters recommendation in that "The foundations of diverse ethical systems include: intuitionism, rationalism, caring and God's divine word."[109]

Our goal as Christians should be to create a better world. Not just for us, but for the generation that come after us as well. We have to hold on to the hope that the world is still full of endless possibilities. We must be willing to dream big, and be courageous enough to do big things. We must be willing to extend ourselves and our resources to communities that do not have. As we have discovered in this text, building better communities is the first step to building a better world. Every day we are given a fresh start to make a difference and impact in the world. Each day we are faced with the options to turn a blind eye to the oppressive environments of the world, and the marginalized, or to become a part of the liberation and freedom

---

[109] Carter, Lawrence Edward, George David Miller, and Neelakanta Radhakrishnan. 2001. *Global Ethical Options*. Trumbull: Weatherhill.

process. As Henri Nouwen states, It is this new world that fills our dreams, guides our actions, and makes us go on, at great risk, with the increasing conviction that one day we will finally be free-free to love![110] There is hope for a world where homicide is not present. There is hope for a day where terrorism with cease. There is hope for a time in history where we love people for who they are and not for their condition. There is the faith that homeless populations will dry up and that a cure for HIV will be discovered. There is hope that God's presence is still here and that God's compassion is still strong for His creations.

---

[110] Nouwen, Henri J. M. 1972. *The Wounded Healer: Ministry in Contemporary Society.* New York: Doubleday Religion.

DEVELOPING CHRIST CONSCIOUSNESS

If contemporary Christians want to become people who are relevant we must primarily become people that are relational. But not just relational in the element and sense of engaging people; we must be willing to engage the social issues that affect people. One of the primary displays of Jesus' ministry was centered on Social Justice. If contemporary Christians want to truly become the heartbeat of God we must be willing to go deep into the environments and areas of the marginalized that Jesus made himself present in. Matthew 9:9-13 is a primary example where we see Jesus as an advocate for relationship building:

> [9] As Jesus was walking along, he saw a man named Matthew sitting at his tax collector's booth. "Follow me and be my disciple," Jesus said to him. So Matthew got up and followed him. [10] Later, Matthew invited Jesus and his disciples to his home as dinner guests, along with many tax collectors and other disreputable sinners. [11] But when the Pharisees saw this, they asked his disciples, "Why does your teacher eat with such scum?" [12] When Jesus heard this, he said, "Healthy people don't need a doctor—sick people do." [13] Then he added, "Now go and learn the meaning of this Scripture: 'I want you to show mercy, not offer sacrifices.' For I have come to call not those who think they are righteous, but those who know they are sinners."

The heart is an organ that is located deep in the rib cage. Therefore, the heartbeat can be found deep in the anatomy of the human body. Utilizing this same analogy, the heart of God is located deep in the center of social issues and injustices. Likewise, the sound of God's heart should be positioned deep in the anatomy of

Christian service. Becoming the heartbeat of God is determined by where we place ourselves in the body of mankind. The body of Christ has a function in the workings of the world. The heart, because of what flows through it, connects every organ, muscle, tissue and atom in the body. The same holds true for True Christians. Because of the message that flows through the gospel, and the connection we have with the blood of Christ as our advocate for salvation, millennial Christians have the ability to connect communities and environments. In the same way Jesus enlightened us to a new consciousness through Old Testament thought, we now have the responsibility to expand New Testament thought in order to enlighten present day thinkers.

The Prophet Isaiah maps out our responsibility as Christians inside of his prophetic writings. Isaiah 1:17 reads for us, *"Learn to do good; seek justice, correct oppression; bring justice to the fatherless, plead the widow's case."* He sums up, in my opinion, the main idea of this text. He also gives us five clear directives that we can utilize as points of departure for the work ahead. The most challenging part of this text is located beyond the first four words Isaiah gives us. We are all taught as children to do good. On the playground, in our classrooms, and in the workplace we are all challenged to do things that are upright. One of the primary messages of the Christian faith is to do kind things, and to behave in such a way that brings honor to our creator. Doing good is easy. It is easy to identify 'good things' a person can do with their lives and for others. We can all come up with a list actions that could qualify us as good people. It is easy to give your time and money to projects as good deeds. Some Christians will read this text, in its totality, and make the cognizant decision to exercise every element of the author's words. However, a True Christian won't stop at "Learn to do good".

As we begin the discussion on developing the consciousness of Christ we should keep in mind that this consciousness is ever evolving and expanding within itself. I would challenge modern Christians to have the faith in this consciousness to drive us into the next phase of humanitarian and social enlightenment. Gandhi says that it is faith that steers us through stormy seas, faith that moves mountains and faith that jumps across the ocean. That faith is nothing but a living, wide-awake consciousness of God within. He who has achieved that faith wants nothing. Bodily diseased, he is spiritually healthy; physically poor, he rolls in spiritual riches.[111] I believe that it will be this Christ consciousness that will guide the church and Christianity back to a place of global relevancy. This is the consciousness needed to help us navigate through the conditions and issues that continue to plague our world. This consciousness will give us the wisdom needed to create change in society. This consciousness, if rooted in the energy of God, will give us the power to transcend obstacles and systems that have perpetuated the oppression and marginalization we see today. The moment we see ourselves as blessed because we are simply alive is the moment we begin to live as Christ.

I was introduced to the concept of Christ Consciousness while I was doing my undergraduate studies at Morehouse College. I had always heard of the idea to think like Christ, but I have never been introduced to developing a personal consciousness of Christ. I had read Philippians 2:5-11 on countless occasions but never understood it's root lesson:

> [5]Let this mind be in you, which was also in Christ Jesus: [6]Who, being in the form of God, thought it not robbery to be equal with God: [7]But made himself of no reputation, and took upon him the form of a servant, and was made in the likeness of men: [8]And being found in fashion as a man, he humbled himself, and became obedient unto death, even the death of the cross. [9]Wherefore God also hath highly exalted him, and given him a name which is above every name: [10]That at the name of Jesus every knee should bow, of things in heaven, and things in earth, and things under the earth; [11]And that every tongue should confess that Jesus Christ is Lord, to the glory of God the Father.

---

[111] Kripalani, Krishna. 2004. *Mahatma Gandhi: All Men Are Brothers Autobiographical Reflections.* New York: The Continuum International Publishing Group.

While many proclaimers of the gospel will stop at verse five we cannot remove its separation from the corresponding versus which help us to see Christ consciousness acted out with humility and care for others. If we were to look at this text in the context of this writing we could note that the root of Christ consciousness is found in our efforts to become like Christ: divine in nature yet compassionate towards the natural. This is probably the greatest struggle many people face today; having the ability to balance between their human nature and their divine nature. As Dean Carter points out, "The pangs of conscience arise when we believe that we can improve a situation but haven't tried to. If my daughter is illiterate and I find illiteracy to be an unsatisfactory condition, then conscience dictates that I should do something to rectify the situation.[112] It is common to become frustrated when a person believes that they have a spiritual assignment from God, yet they do not see the physical resources in order to make it happen. There are huge tasks in the world that need to be corrected and rectified. To embrace the consciousness of Christ there should be a willingness to go after solutions that have yet to be attempted. Through the example of Jesus we see a fearless champion who was unafraid to go face to face with the religious consciousness that placed hindrances on His community.

I would like to introduce you to Dean Lawrence Carter's recommendations for how we can develop this Christ consciousness. What he says in his text mirrors what has been said in the biblical text. Ephesians 4:11-12 offer us the original model for consideration: "[11]And he gave some, apostles; and some, prophets; and some, evangelists; and some, pastors and teachers; [12]For the perfecting of the saints, for the work of the ministry, for the edifying of the body of Christ:" We all have gifts, talents, resources, connections, networks, ideas and energy that can be turned over to God for the improvement of humanity. God placed these gifts within us to be used by us. Paul points out in verse 12 that there are three specific tasks we should consider:

---

[112] Carter, Lawrence Edward, George David Miller, and Neelakanta Radhakrishnan. 2001. *Global Ethical Options*. Trumbull: Weatherhill.

1. Helping people become better people, 2. Helping to advance the message of Christ and Christianity, and 3. Caring to the needs of humanity. Dr. Carter words his position in the following way by stating, "Ethical improvement occurs in three fundamental ways: 1. Improvement of self, 2. Improvement of Others, 3. Collective Improvement of All Beings."[113]

To embrace Christ consciousness would entail that we are making the cognizant effort to become better individuals. It would also imply that we are more aware of our responsibility to help others become all that God has called them to be. Finally, according to Dr. Carter, to embrace this level of consciousness would entail our commitment to being the human agents commissioned to work for the enhancements of the communities we have been called to serve. One cannot simply say "I am Christ conscious" without having the knowledge of what this title requires of them.

What the Christ Conscious person also understands is that their enlightenment will come from their total involvement with the world around them. Harrison Elliot points out that, "Progressive religious educators gave us an important place to continuous manifestations of God in nature and in human life. Nature and history are also manifestations of God who becomes known only through the experience and relevant search of men and women."[114] In our efforts to connect to the oppressed and the marginalized communities of today, one may have to revisit these communities of our past. What can be observed is that many of these communities of people have been in existence since the beginning of time. We can also point out that the issues of the world have been the issues of humanity since the time of Adam and Eve. What happens when we tap into the communities of the past

---

[113] Carter, Lawrence Edward, George David Miller, and Neelakanta Radhakrishnan. 2001. *Global Ethical Options.* Trumbull: Weatherhill.

[114] Elliott, Harrison S. 1940. *Can Religious Education Be Christian?* New York: Macmillan.

is we stumble upon the champions that came before us simultaneously. There are various things we can learn from those who embraced this consciousness before us. We can learn from their mistakes. We can gleam from their successes. But ultimately we trace our present Christ Consciousness back to the God consciousness that formed the world in the beginning. Before Jesus Christ made us aware of the oppressed and the marginalized, God Himself advocated for the burdened and the disregarded.

I would challenge you to make it your goal to embrace the pages that follow. I would admonish you to search within for the Christ that is inside of you. To the same degree I would encourage you to search for the Christ within others. I believe that God is searching for people who are willing to set their agendas and mindsets about the world aside and focus on developing a better world. Elliott also states that:

> "There should be more sense of social responsibility and a larger consciousness of social sin. This gives the basis for a realistic religious education which recognizes fully the limitations of human beings and the seriousness of the human problem, but, at the same time, renders it possible to make a positive attack upon the problems through the educative process.[115]

The world will not do better until it knows better. It cannot know better until someone, or something, makes them aware. That awareness should spawn action. I agree that social sin is real, and that is our Christian responsibility to bring salvation as an option. However, this can only take place when those who have fully embraced their Christ consciousness begin to raise the consciousness of others.

This will involve bridging new gaps and building new community networks. However, history has proven to us that when we come together with like minds, or

---

[115] Elliott, Harrison S. 1940. *Can Religious Education Be Christian?* New York: Macmillan.

consciousness, anything is possible. The bible supports this idea that transformation and revolution begin at the place called the mind. Romans 12:1-3 says:

> "¹And so, dear brothers and sisters, I plead with you to give your bodies to God because of all he has done for you. Let them be a living and holy sacrifice—the kind he will find acceptable. This is truly the way to worship him. ²Don't copy the behavior and customs of this world, but let God transform you into a new person by changing the way you think. Then you will learn to know God's will for you, which is good and pleasing and perfect. ³Because of the privilege and authority God has given me, I give each of you this warning: Don't think you are better than you really are. Be honest in your evaluation of yourselves, measuring yourselves by the faith God has given us."

This collective consciousness creates, what I like to call, community consciousness. As we embrace our individual responsibilities we create groups of people who share the same compassion for the world. I believe this is what Jesus' end desire was for the world He lived in. He wanted people to feel a personal conviction that would light a fire for community consciousness. Henri Nouwen supports this community consciousness when he says, "There we experience ourselves no longer as isolated individuals caught in the diabolic chain of cause and effect, but as beings able to transcend the fences of our own predicament and to reach out far beyond the concerns of self. There we touch the place where all people are revealed as equal and where compassion becomes a human possibility."[116] Love for humanity is possible. Grace and mercy received by the oppressed and the marginalized is possible. Hope to communities that have been giving life changing circumstances is possible. The reallocation of personal, and universal, resources is possible. The eradication of racism, hatred, bigotry and genocide are all possible. Access to healthcare and clean running water is possible. The construction of affordable housing for those who live

---

[116] Nouwen, Henri J. M. 1972. *The Wounded Healer: Ministry in Contemporary Society.* New York: Doubleday Religion.

below the poverty line is possible. Offering a person the option of work in exchange for selling their body in the human sex trafficking industry is possible.

We should not be shocked as the disciples were in the book of Matthew 19:25-26 where they ask Jesus the question regarding who can be delivered from their present state of reality. The bible states, "[25]The disciples were astounded. "Then who in the world can be saved?" they asked. [26]Jesus looked at them intently and said, "Humanly speaking, it is impossible. But with God everything is possible." We should know longer be asking God the question "who can be saved?" The question of the person who has embraced their fullest Christ consciousness will ask the question "who can I help be saved?"

GOOD WON'T GET IT

Unfortunately, just being a Good Christian will turn you into an irrelevant Christian.

As we analyze the previous mentioned text we can note that it is what we read beyond "Learn to do good" that requires True Christians to engage with humanity and get dirty! Beyond the first four words of this text we can imply that doing good is not good enough. In order to seek justice we must go looking for opportunities that need our moral compass. It has always amazed me at the level of resources the church and Christians have, yet we have to be propositioned before doing anything with those resources. Churches sit on millions of dollars in membership giving with no intent to use that money to better humanity. They would rather budget that money to hire more staff and build more buildings. Why can't Christians be the ones running to the front line for service? Why are we not banging down the doors of organizations and initiatives to discover their needs? Why is it so hard to partner financial, and people, support to the causes of the community?

Some may be curious as to why my views towards Christians and the modern church have become so critical. Why am I offering such a strong critique regarding the relevancy of this faith community? The truth is that it has nothing to do with Christian or church actions. It is actually connected with Christian's non-action on social issues. From my current perspective, I know there are countless organizations and movements who have requested the help and partnership of churches only to be told at the front desk, "we already have something like that here" by the church receptionist.

As the biblical writing states, it is our responsibility to "correct oppression" and "bring justice". To correct and to bring both require action on the Christian faith and those who profess Christianity. I am of the personal belief many of today's Christians are afraid to correct oppression because we are too afraid to call out the oppressors in the community! Many of today's Christians are fearful to usher in justice for all. Why? Because this process would entail bucking and demolishing the systems that perpetuate the injustices. It will take courage to accomplish these tasks, but what better soldier for humanity than a soldier for God?

There are some major elements I believe Jesus wanted each of us to consider. We should consider these recommendations not solely as our Christian duty, but as our human obligation to the world. Even if you do not identify yourself as a Christian, or person of religious affiliation, there should be some moral pull on your consciousness to do good for others. Whether you attend Sunday morning worship or prefer the more contemporary evening fellowships there should be a pull in your heart towards service. Whether your religious leader preaches a 45 minute sermon on Sunday mornings, or offers a 25 minute life lesson, there should be a fire within you the burns for the birth of a better world. As Dean Lawrence Carter states, Conscience compels us to look beyond what is simply convenient or fashionable.[117] When we embrace the true sense of Christ consciousness we will understand that it will require sacrifice and unpopularity.

I can see this term Christ Consciousness becoming a popular, or fad, word. I can see people using this term to sound intellectually astute and spiritually in tune with the world. I can see people using this phrase as a way to suggest that they have been enlightened as a Christian or as a religious leader. I would urge these bandwagon riders to use caution if they choose to associate their selves with this term. For to make this claim it will come at a high cost in the eyes of God. To speak that you seek to gain the same awareness Jesus had for the world, while He was present on earth, carries a certain weight along with it.

---

[117] Carter, Lawrence Edward, George David Miller, and Neelakanta Radhakrishnan. 2001. *Global Ethical Options*. Trumbull: Weatherhill.

For a person to say they are spiritually conscious is a lofty declaration within itself. To tact on the term, and association with, Christ magnifies its definition tremendously. Dean Lawrence Carter taught me that, "Conscience is derived from the Latin term conscientia, coined by Cicero to describe how the inner voice, not public approval, dictates ethical action. In other words the intention to act or reflection after action is followed by a moment of negation and concluded by the awareness of moral principles."[118] The bible makes mention of this small inner voice in 1 Kings 19:9-12 as God speaks to Elijah:

> "But the lord said to him, "What are you doing here, Elijah?" [10]Elijah replied, "I have zealously served the lord God Almighty. But the people of Israel have broken their covenant with you, torn down your altars, and killed every one of your prophets. I am the only one left, and now they are trying to kill me, too." [11]"Go out and stand before me on the mountain," the lord told him. And as Elijah stood there, the lord passed by, and a mighty windstorm hit the mountain. It was such a terrible blast that the rocks were torn loose, but the lord was not in the wind. After the wind there was an earthquake, but the lord was not in the earthquake. [12]And after the earthquake there was a fire, but the lord was not in the fire. And after the fire there was the sound of a gentle whisper."

I think it is safe to correlate the small voice within to the voice of God. I believe the small voice that is calling us to be champions of change is the voice of God. The inner voice that has made us aware of the social injustices and has charged us to make a difference is the voice of God. The inner voice that dialogues with our morals and right considerations, and judgements, is the voice of God. Christ consciousness is an extension of God consciousness. It is God's voice that pushes us into new heights and challenges us to go deep into the dark communities of the marginalized and the oppressed. If we are in question if this is the voice of God, we can parallel the request with the uncomfortability of the response. As Dean Lawrence Carter further states, "Conscience compels people to challenge the status quo and

---

[118] Carter, Lawrence Edward, George David Miller, and Neelakanta Radhakrishnan. 2001. *Global Ethical Options*. Trumbull: Weatherhill.

promote justice. It also compels people to place themselves in harm's way of retaliation from the established order."[119] In more precise terms, if the voice you hear is pushing you into the uncomfortable it is more than likely the voice of God.

I had the distinct honor to sit down with Dr. Carter in my post seminary experience to discuss his book as well as to discuss his current thoughts about ethical actions in the world. It had been close to ten years since I sat under his professorship, but I want to thank him for the time he spent with me to dialogue regarding this text's topic. In an interview with Dean Lawrence E. Carter, of The Martin Luther King Jr. International Chapel at Morehouse College he stated:

> "There is the necessity of competency. We must be steadfast, honest and true to our commitment. Sustained reflection, the courage to love and the will to act. Autonomy is an ingredient of freedom. It is not self sufficiency. We have the freedom to choose to conform or not. We must be willing to be the last one standing for change like King. We must be conscious no to segregate our moral conscious. When you practice a social awareness of diversity you must be willing to address the myriad of issues. We have to be self initiating to combat and address the structures of society. Chose goals and move harmoniously towards one common goal. We cannot accept our authority and responsibility to act unconditionally. Affirmative reflection value creates action. It is only through self transcendence that we can be guided to the levels of the ideals. Our moral action helps us to reach this transcendence. Keeping in mind that it is our ideals that guide our behavior. The moral life is about keeping the faith while we make these changes in humanity, and ultimately our self. Persons are responsible to themselves. One can be morally immature. The pains of conscious are caused by the call of obligation."[120]

---

[119] Carter, Lawrence Edward, George David Miller, and Neelakanta Radhakrishnan. 2001. *Global Ethical Options*. Trumbull: Weatherhill.

[120] Rev. Dr. Lawrence E. Carter, Sr., interview by Dr. Wendel T. Dandridge. 2016. *Dean of The Martin Luther King Jr. International Ecumenical Chapel on the Campus of Morehouse College* (April 19).

JESUS' CALL TO ACTION

Jesus was calling True Christians to action. We cannot define ourselves as Christians if we are not on the move. If we are not going out into the world and reaching the masses we are falling short of the great commission of Christ. One consistency in Jesus' ministry was that he was always on the move. Jesus never stayed because Jesus understood that to stay still would imply complacency. He traveled from city to city because he understood the bigness of his mission. What He understood was that his commission from His Father was to reach as many as he could with the message of hope and love. Jesus understood that a true example of being God's heartbeat on earth would require action and momentum. I believe Jesus was frustrated with the 'word' of the synagogue and wanted to see people acting out the gospel, or good news of God. To the same point, I believe people are tired of hearing the talk of Christians and want to see Christians walk the walk they profess. What Jesus saw in bible days, I believe, has only perpetuated itself in modern day: idle people who are comfortable being Christian but are uncomfortable doing the work of Christ. Jesus championed a call to action during his time on earth. I would like to do the same! **I am calling True Christians from their places of idleness and challenging them to act on the issues that still plague humanity.**

It is interesting to note when we see Jesus interacting with religious leaders, and magistrates, they often challenged Him with the written text. Often they would attempt to pull Old Testament consciousness to trump the consciousness of Christ. Jesus' reply would always call people to act on what they were taught with the consideration to its effects on the present. Jesus also challenged the thinkers of the day to re-evaluate how they did ministry. Jesus created a movement while modern Christians have became comfortable with studying and learning about His words. If we are going to be true Christians we must be willing to move into the areas and environments that need our action and support. It never ceases to amaze me the number of Christians who are content sitting in the chairs of church with no desire to get up and walk into humanity as game changers.

Most orthodox Christians can tell you what the bible says. The Christians who attend worship on a weekly basis, but won't attend a community service function, can tell you what the Pastor preached on Sunday (if they weren't sleep), but can't articulate the current social issues that plague humanity. Church attending Christians can tell you how to live "right" but can't outline a list of service opportunities for you to participate in. Some Christians can give you the dos and the don'ts of life without offering the does and don'ts of engagement for specific oppressed and marginalized communities. Common Christians can quote litanies and hymns but can't recite the bills and laws that keep people from rising through society. Some Christians will always be present in vacation bible school but refuse to tutor children who live in communities where afterschool educational options are not available. A few Christians will always be present in bible study and Sunday morning worship, but will never attend a Friday night homeless feeding. Comparable to bible days, there will be some Christians who will always be in the synagogue reading the scribes but refuse to read up on the current happenings of the globe and how these happenings effect our community. My question is when will True Christians choose to show up in the same environments of the oppressed and the marginalized and make humanitarian change? Where are the Christians who feel the pull to be different from the religious practitioners who came before them?

What Mary Daly says brings us to the realization that, "Why indeed must "God" be a noun? Why not a verb? – the most active and dynamic of all?"[121] In other words, the God of present time is not confined to being a person, place or thing. Who

---

[121] Carter, Lawrence Edward, George David Miller, and Neelakanta Radhakrishnan. 2001. *Global Ethical Options*. Trumbull: Weatherhill.

God is, in the present world, can be seen through the actions of the change agents we call Christians.

We can no longer place God in the box of understanding. The truth is that we will never know God in His totality until we meet Him face to face. We will never experience the highest form of God consciousness until we meet our creator. To the same extent we will never experience the totality of God on earth, because God's extensions on earth are but finite and human. However, this does not negate that God's presence, or Christ's consciousness, is minimalized. Aristotle suggests that we "assume the end and consider how and by what means it is to be attained; and if it seems to be produced by several means they consider by which it is most easily and best produced."[122] God's desire for the world may be singular in nature, however the vessels God will use to get the task done will be numerous. We must remember that the ultimate goal is universal love and community service. There are innumerable ways to make this possibility a reality. To connect to the consciousness of Christ is to understand that each environment is unique and will require distinctive strategies and people to get the task done. Therefore, God will use a "by any means necessary" approach to produce the more perfect world He desires.

Henri Nouwen further suggests that, "None of us can offer leadership to anyone unless we make our presence known- that is, unless we step forward out of the anonymity and apathy of our surroundings and make the possibility of fellowship visible."[123] The church, and Christianity, cannot be leaders for social and community change until they make the intentional act to be that trailblazer and pioneer for humanity. Both the church universal and the Christian must make their existence, and

---

[122] Aristotle. 1997. *Nichomachean Ethics.* London: Wordsworth.

[123] Nouwen, Henri J. M. 1972. *The Wounded Healer: Ministry in Contemporary Society.* New York: Doubleday Religion.

influence, felt in the workings and happenings of social and community change. I strongly believe that to regain relevancy, the church, and Christianity, will need to place its bare feet on the heated coals of the hot topics that are prevalent in today's culture. They can no longer take the back seat as speakers for change but not doers of justice. People need to see Christians being Christians.

People need to see more Christians going after the forgotten. If we only knew the power of our actions to our onlookers. For to act does not solely bring awareness to those who are in the position to create change, it also speaks a message to the communities who are waiting for change to come to them. Many of the previous mentioned groups in this text feel as though the world has forgotten about them. They feel as though they are isolated to the point of no return. Many of them feel as though their present condition is the final reality. However what we have come to discover is the power of hope when these communities see the rescue team getting into position for social battle. Henri Nouwen says that, "Human beings can keep their sanity and stay alive as long as there is at least one person waiting for them. But when "nothing and nobody" is waiting, there is no chance to survive in the struggle for life."[124] When we make the conscious decision to act we send a surge of hope to those who feel as though they have been overlooked. I see this every Friday night on the streets of Atlanta, and when my church sponsors community initiatives. People make the choice to live, and endure, because they know someone is coming to their rescue. We must choose to be God's rescue team.

---

[124] Nouwen, Henri J. M. 1972. *The Wounded Healer: Ministry in Contemporary Society.* New York: Doubleday Religion.

JESUS AS A CHAMPION FOR SOCIAL JUSTICE

Jesus was a human who championed social justice. The primary message of Jesus was to raise the awareness of social issues in the communities He frequented. Outside of Jesus' believed divinity and miracle workings, we cannot throw out the fact that Jesus was a human who advocated for change and communal fairness. Jesus was a man who fought for the humanity of other men, and women. Jesus saw, even in his era, that there was a need for a voice that advocated for the marginalized and the disenfranchised. Jesus took the lead when others were afraid. Jesus associated Himself with those who were ostracized by the status quo.

From the story of the Good Samaritan to the woman who was caught in adultery, Jesus identified the wrongs of the world and gave recommendations for a new way of human agency. In these specific examples, Jesus calls for the community to uphold the autonomous value of the individual and not to focus on the condition of the person. His example, and actions, were out of the norm. Jesus not only showed he was connected to the people, He also demonstrated through his words, his feelings about some of the social dynamics in His city.

As a Rabbi, or religious teacher, Jesus was well aware of the religious law and how it should be executed. Jesus was well aware that His actions would stir up concern and dissatisfaction from the church and other religious leaders. Jesus was well versed on the divide between communities and classes. Jesus was cognizant of how his interactions with the poor, the adulterer, the prostitute, the fisherman and the tax collectors would influence his reputation. Jesus knew that "his kind" wasn't to associate themselves with the communities listed above. Nevertheless Jesus realized His voice had the power to shift the nations and to change the consciousness of the world. It is a shame other religious leaders, who have innumerable ears at their attention each week, refuse to use their platform to inform the masses about the inequalities that are still prevalent in the world.

Historically speaking, a person cannot negate why Jesus was killed. Christians have come to believe Jesus' death was for salvation and their sins. We have also come to believe that Jesus was killed because of his religious teachings and miracles. While these philosophies are valid in their own right, the truth is that Jesus was processed through the judicial system for his stance on community issues and the church's involvement in social issues. Jesus was killed because He was shifting the norm and calling out the wrongs of humanity.

Let's call a spade a spade, Jesus was a trouble maker. Jesus wasn't liked. There were numerous times where the actions of Jesus caused a bit of ruckus during his travels. But then again it wasn't just for what He displayed during his travels, it was also a matter of what He said. Jesus said things that went perpendicular to the voices that came before him. Jesus said things that raised the personal consciousness of all who listened. If we are going to be champions for social justice, as Jesus was, we cannot be afraid to utilize our voices. We can't be so focused on doing a good deed that we forget to dialogue with the environments to which the good deed is being executed. Change doesn't take place exclusively through the actions of a community. True change happens when leaders, and other influential persons, get together and begin dialogue about a process involving an implementation strategy for solutions.

Jesus died because Jesus was creating societal and community change; not because he was building a church or religious movement.

We have to remember that the true victory of the cross was because Jesus proved that to sacrifice for another would bring us closer to our creator. What Jesus taught us while here on earth was that to die for a cause was the ultimate conduit to raise the consciousness of the community. What the cross teaches us is that we can be victorious when we choose to stay true to our earthly assignments that are divine in nature. As Dean Lawrence Carter states, "The moral arc of the universe bends towards justice. In the final analysis, goodness will triumph."[125] Jesus teaches us that love triumphs all and that compassion wins over evil.

We must have the faith that our actions will right the wrongs and injustices of society. True Christians have an assurance that God's word stands as the ultimate authority for moral transformation. The scriptures we find in the bible have been time tested and divinely approved. The power we find in the bible gives us the strength we need to champion these social and humanitarian causes. However the modern millennial Christian must be confident in this truth. Failure to believe in this truth, and stand on the promises of God, is to accept defeat. Dr. Carter supports me when he says:

> Much of the wind is taken from our ethical sails if we believe our actions will not lead to the righting of wrongs:
>
> 1. Our work with the homeless is more meaningful if we believe that our actions will one day lead to the end of homelessness,
>
> 2. We are better able to make sacrifices for a clean and safe environment if we are convinced they will be lead to clean and safe world, and
>
> 3. The deaths of people for the cause of world peace mean little if we do not believe that their deaths contribute to world peace in the future.[126]

The ideas in this text are not just for Christian consideration. All who share and occupy this space called earth have some things to consider. Love and compassion is not just for the Baptist or the Pentecostal. This universal truth of altruistic work should be present in the thread of all faith practices and dogmas.

---

[125] Carter, Lawrence Edward, George David Miller, and Neelakanta Radhakrishnan. 2001. *Global Ethical Options*. Trumbull: Weatherhill.

[126] Carter, Lawrence Edward, George David Miller, and Neelakanta Radhakrishnan. 2001. *Global Ethical Options*. Trumbull: Weatherhill.

Joseph Gremillion shows that this is reflected in Vatican II's Pastoral Constitution on the Church in the Modern World and boldly articulated in this key statement from the 1971 Synod document "Justice in the World":

> "Action on behalf of justice and participation in the transformation of the world fully appear to us as a constitutive dimension of the preaching of the Gospel, or, in other words, of the Church's mission for the redemption of the human race and its liberation from every oppressive situation.[127]

The proclamation of God's word is meant to do more than excite people during community worship. God's word was intended to motivate people to a place of action. God's word was proposed to bring hope in hopeless environments. To advocate for justice in the world is to open the bible and read from the lips of God.

As I have stated before, we are responsible and will be held accountable for the impact we have made on earth. We cannot continue to observe the problems facing the world and do nothing about it. Our unwillingness to respond to these issues only perpetuate the problem. In my opinion non-action is a sin. Non-action keeps us separated from God. For to act on these issues would bring us closer to God. Henri Nouwen suggests that "Many people are convinced that there is something terribly wrong with the world in which they live and feel that cooperation with existing models of living constitutes a kind of betrayal of the self.[128] We see this attitude towards action throughout the course of history. We see communities from the days of Moses, to Dr. Martin Luther King, to the present Mother of the Movement, who have echoed that to stand by and do nothing is to propagate the injustices. Moses said he could not live in Pharaoh's house as long as he continued to mistreat the Hebrew slaves.

---

[127] Gremillion, Joseph. 1976. *The Gospel of Peace and Justice: Catholic Social Teaching Since Pope John.* Maryknoll: Orbis.

[128] Nouwen, Henri J. M. 1972. *The Wounded Healer: Ministry in Contemporary Society.* New York: Doubleday Religion.

Dr. King said that he could not sit idle in Atlanta while people in Mississippi and Birmingham were being lynched and burned alive. The Mothers of the Movement have said that together they will stand to stop law enforcement brutality and error. We too should be willing to take stands against the injustices that are present in our community. To do nothing about the issues, mentioned previously in this text, along with those unlisted, is to preserve their existence.

JESUS' PUSH FOR EQUALITY

Jesus believed in equality. Jesus was the personification of God meeting people on their level. Jesus, as the Son of God, hung out with the "least of them". God incarnate came to earth to prove that, even He, can humble Himself to be equal (on the same level) as man. The problem Jesus had with the environment he lived in was the hierarchal system that was tearing humanity apart because of their differences. Jesus was tired of people thinking of themselves as higher than the humility of God.

No two people are the same. God created each of us uniquely. To the same degree no two people carry the same qualifications for all environments. This does not mean we have to view someone else as other than human. We should appreciate the differences and individuality of all of God's creations. Jesus' greatest tension was trying to understand why people were viewed so differently when we are all, at the core, human. Jesus brought to the forefront of people's mind that we are all united by the same breath that was breathed into Adam at the beginning of time. I want it to be clear that equality does not mean everyone necessarily being the same and on the same level. What equality means, in my opinion and the context of this text, is that each person should be placed on the same level of **value** as the other. Jesus never advocated that everyone should be the same. Jesus, however, gave a compelling example of how everyone should be **treated** the same; with love and dignity.

Society created the pods of magistrates, Sadducees, Pharisees, Priest, tax collectors, prostitutes and the sick of Jesus' era. Likewise, current systems have created groups of people that we embrace as less than the other. It has been made evident in the scriptures that each of these pods had their own communities. In today's culture we can observe the same. What can be witnessed in history is that there was to be no comingling between any of these groups. Today we still see this same separation between the free and the marginalized. **Jesus breaks the system of inequality by inviting everyone to eat at the same table.** When you examine the occupations of the twelve disciples you will discover that Jesus was trying to get us to understand that no person has more, or greater value, than another person. Jesus' inner circle of followers were a mix-match gathering of people. The crowds Jesus spoke to consisted of the common town resident, and not just those who attended worship in the synagogue. Jesus offers the poor to sit with the rich and the sick to sit with the well. This practice should still be our point of departure today.

When will we be like Jesus and invite the fisherman, the tax collector, the bookkeeper and the Zealot together? When will we be like Jesus and invite the Muslim, the single mother, the prostitute, the person living with HIV and the felon to the same table to eat? The table is spread and the feast is plentiful. Modern millennial Christians should be more than willing, and open, to extend the same invitation to the table that Jesus extended to the oppressed and the marginalized of His day.

HOW JESUS BRINGS LIGHT TO THE REAL ISSUES OF HUMANITY AND COMMUNITY

Jesus believed that social issues are real issues. The issues of today are not figments of our imagination. The problems we face in the world are not things that will just go away on their own over time. Jesus' message challenges us not to separate ourselves from, what I would like to call, "the other". The issue I find with most modern Christians is they are focused on the wrong issues. I would almost venture to say that modern Christians aren't focused on any social and humanitarian issues at all. Christianity has become one of those things that has caused many people, after joining a church or a fellowship, to put much of their attention into the four walls of the building. Instead we should be looking outward for the subjects we are being challenged to discover solutions for. The true Christian should focus their attention on what their church is doing in their community with the resources God has afforded them.

I believe Jesus' message to the world was for us to focus on humanitarian and global issues, not church problems. We cannot turn a blind eye to the lack of clean water in Ghana as a result of our focus on our soup kitchen in Atlanta. We cannot turn a deaf ear to the cries of children being sold as sex slaves in Brazil because we are too focused on implementing our new Vacation Bible School Curriculum in Baltimore. We can't miss the need to provide food for the homeless because we are focused on the Pastor's Anniversary Banquet. We cannot forget to support the single mother who is living away from her family because we are focused on the next church musical.

Social issues are the real issues we should be grabbing by the bull's horn and riding until our palms are bloody.

The same time and attention we give to church events should be evenly distributed towards community events. The same way we take a full year to plan for church anniversary, we should commit the same time and attention to build a new international project to combat poverty in underdeveloped countries. Modern Christians should begin the process of what I like to call "focus inversion" in the church. Instead of the lens centering to the altar of the sanctuary, we should be out building altars (places that suggest the presence of God) outside the church. The attention of the Christian should be far from meeting budgets and planning conferences. Instead, it should be on community agendas and global solution discoveries. The True Christians voice can't just be heard in the pulpits; it should be heard on the steps of City Hall. There is a community of Christians who like fads and buzz words. True Christians hear the genuine issues and refuse to cease dialogue until solutions are not just brought to the table but implemented as well. The real issues of Christianity are not religious, or faith issues at all. The true issues for the True Christian are philanthropic in nature.

JESUS' PUSH FOR HUMAN RIGHTS OVER POLITICAL RIGHTS

Jesus believed in human rights over political rights. Jesus believed that human rights and global justice should be harmonious. As I stated before, Jesus was killed because of his conscious-raising actions towards the community and the Jewish faith. This is what would label him an advocate. I would suggest every miracle Jesus performed was preceded by a statement of human rights. Jesus had the mentality, and voice, that spoke "All have the same value as the other". Jesus' message always challenged the idea that even the least are deserving of redemption. Remember his words in Matthew 25:37-40:

> "[37]Then these righteous ones will reply, 'Lord, when did we ever see you hungry and feed you? Or thirsty and give you something to drink? [38]Or a stranger and show you hospitality? Or naked and give you clothing? [39]When did we ever see you sick or in prison and visit you?' [40]"And the King will say, 'I tell you the truth, when you did it to one of the least of these my brothers and sisters, you were doing it to me!'"

While history and communities have always advocated for the separation of church and government, Jesus demonstrated to us a very different ideal. Yes, God's law and man's law can remain separate, however, separate does not mean disassociation. A person's decisions reflect directly on the other. What Jesus showed us is that while the laws can remain separate there can still be dialogue across party lines. What Jesus teaches us is that the priest and the president should be seated at the same table. In order to form better communities, there needs to be a moral element partnered with a system of checks and balances. There should be leadership in place that can uphold the laws of the land as well as uphold an ethical, and divine, standard for humanity. Jesus was never directly against government. In truth, the Bible advises us to honor government officials and to revere them as elected by God:

> "[1]Everyone must submit to governing authorities. For all authority comes from God, and those in positions of authority have been placed there by God. [2]So anyone who rebels against authority is rebelling against what God has instituted, and they will be punished. [3]For the authorities do not strike fear in people who are doing right,

but in those who are doing wrong. Would you like to live without fear of the authorities? Do what is right, and they will honor you. ⁴The authorities are God's servants, sent for your good. But if you are doing wrong, of course you should be afraid, for they have the power to punish you. They are God's servants, sent for the very purpose of punishing those who do what is wrong. ⁵So you must submit to them, not only to avoid punishment, but also to keep a clear conscience. ⁶Pay your taxes, too, for these same reasons. For government workers need to be paid. They are serving God in what they do. ⁷Give to everyone what you owe them: Pay your taxes and government fees to those who collect them, and give respect and honor to those who are in authority. (Romans 13:1-7)

What Jesus did not 100% support was the "government of the church". What he saw was people who thought themselves above the law and wanted to be "God's Judges" here on earth. Jesus utilized his voice to make sure all were treated as human. The message I believe Jesus wanted each of us to model was that there is no government system, or otherwise, that can place value on an individual. We are all God's children, and because of that we should all be treated with the highest esteem and regard.

Please do not misinterpret my exegesis of the biblical scriptures. Jesus did believe Government should be in place and that all government has been ordained by God. Nevertheless, there is a difference in the implementation of rules and regulations by government; and government determining who has access to certain rights and who doesn't. I believe Jesus' message addressed the latter of the two. We cannot identify what "human rights" are until we come the understanding of what "human" is. We cannot keep pushing social and community issues until we have a clear Christ Consciousness about our responsibility to the person.

We must believe that the world has the potential to be a better place. There should be a belief that inequalities can be corrected with the help of God and the policies we have in place in our governments. We should seek to improve the world and everything that makes up society. Policies, laws and orders should be revisited often for the sake of improvement. Dr. Lawrence Carter echoes my sentiments when he states, "The improvement principle is rooted in the belief that the world is transformable. It also extends beyond the individual to the collective improvement of humanity."[129] When we embrace humanity over policies and political agendas the world becomes more communal. The Christians of today should have the faith that the world has the potential to renovate itself through the word of God. It will require communities to create communities and leaders from faith environments, as well as government officials, to make the world a better place.

Gandhi declares that each human life, together with its environment, partakes of the fundamental life force of the entire cosmos. It follows, that any change in the life condition of a single human being can, in the inner reaches of life itself, exert an influence on other human lives. And since nature and the cosmos are living entities, the waves emanating from one human life can not only shake the foundation of other living beings, but can affect things usually thought to be lifeless.[130] To revive the relevancy of the church, and the faith, there ought to be a willingness to cooperate with the systems around us. There should be a clear understanding that the laws that are put in place in one part of the world have an effect on the quality of life for others in distant communities. What can be learned from the message and model of Jesus is that at the end of the day community initiatives trump political progress. If what we choose to pass in our governments continue to keep people oppressed and marginalized we cannot call ourselves advocates of change. On the other hand, if we are willing to work with government to change, and eradicate, social policies and systems we become workers for, and with, Christ.

---

[129] Carter, Lawrence Edward, George David Miller, and Neelakanta Radhakrishnan. 2001. *Global Ethical Options*. Trumbull: Weatherhill.

[130] Carter, Lawrence Edward, George David Miller, and Neelakanta Radhakrishnan. 2001. *Global Ethical Options*. Trumbull: Weatherhill.

JESUS: A MAN FOR THE OPPRESSED

Jesus was a man for the oppressed. It is easy for us to point the finger at the current social issues happening in our world. However I would like to ask how many current Christians are taking that same finger and adding more pressure to the oppressed situations of the world?

There can be no oppression if there is no oppressor.

Jesus refused to be a part of the problem. Jesus refused to be like the other religious leaders of his time who offered critiques of others with no solutions. As Christians, we should also refuse to add to the situational oppression of others. From the days of Moses, until now, we have witnessed a God of the oppressed. Over the course of history it has been clear that God hears the cries of the oppressed communities and has compassion towards their condition. Throughout time we have seen God reveal God's self in the form of liberator for the people. If the term "Messiah" translates as the "promised deliverer" one should pose the question 'to whom does the Messiah come to deliverer'? More importantly, we should be discovering which communities God wants to bring out of oppression today. What has happened over the ages is we have forgotten the true purpose, and need, of God. Humanity cannot save itself. This is the reason God sent an extension of Himself in the form of Jesus. Humanity needs the energy from which it was birthed for redemption. Yet, God thrives off the participation of human agency in the world. Unfortunately, what happened in the days of Moses has reoccurred in the modern day Christendom: oppressed communities are popping up that need liberation from their environments.

What has happened over the course of history is Christians have become the oppressors. Placing judgement on the marginalized is just as immoral as the actions of the person who created the margin. From the days of Moses, and the Exodus story, we have always seen God acting on behalf of the burdened. We have always seen throughout the scriptures a God who has a heart for the oppressed. History has shown us that oppressed communities and people are the populations and individuals who need the most compassion.

When we see the oppressed we should not see an opportunity to get 'Christian brownie points'. When we see the oppressed we should not see a photo op situation. When we see the oppressed we should not see a chance to look like the Super Man/Woman of the day. When we see the oppressed we should not see an opportunity to make ourselves feel better about our lives. Caring for, and tending to the needs of the oppressed, is about answering the question, "How can the love of God be displayed in this environment?" What True Christians bring to any oppressed environment is hope. True Christians have been commissioned to plant seeds in our community that produce the fruits of the spirit: Love, Joy, Peace, Patience, Kindness, Goodness, Faithfulness, Gentleness and Self-Control (Galatians 5:22-23).

I would question why have modern Christians not taken the lead in demonstrating compassion to the modern day oppressed communities? The truth is we have identified these communities. However, our hearts do not bleed for them. The oppression of our brothers and sisters have not touched our hearts to the point that would cause us to act. Outside of the oppressed communities I have listed in this text, there are many other pods of people who suffer from oppression on a daily basis. The component that makes my heart bleed is how some modern Christians have ostracized the oppressed from the community of believers. They are unwelcome in our churches and their voices have been silenced by the general public. If God and Jesus were advocates for compassion towards the oppressed, we should follow suit.

If we are going to exhibit the heartbeat of God on earth we have to be Christians who have empathy towards those who have been cast aside by others. Will we become a people that relieves the pressure of the oppressed instead of adding weight to their burdens?

Reverend Dr. Martin Luther King Jr. says, I still believe that love is the most durable power in the world…what is the summon bonum of life? I think I have discovered the highest good. It is love. This principle stands at the center of the cosmos. As John says, "God is Love". King also says, that I am convinced that we shall overcome because the arc of the universe is long but it bends towards justice.[131]

---

[131] Carter, Lawrence Edward, George David Miller, and Neelakanta Radhakrishnan. 2001. *Global Ethical Options*. Trumbull: Weatherhill.

JESUS: A MAN FOR THE DISINHERITED

Jesus and the disinherited. So often are their people in society that were once a part of the 'inner circle'. Yet one small change in their status caused them to be pushed outside of the group. We have all made mistakes in life. However, some modern Christians, and society, have labeled some situations as non-redemptive. There are those who are viewed as too-far-gone to receive help. This community of people is probably one of the primary groups in need of hope. There are communities of people who were a part of the family who now have become the disinherited.

I am always shocked at the issues, and communities of people, contemporary Christians and modern church refuse to touch and engage. One thing we pride ourselves with at The Worship Center is our willingness to go into the 'dark corners' of ministry. We don't mind setting up a table in the middle of the mall to test people for HIV. We are ok with visiting hotels and street corners where we know people are being sold for sex. We are unafraid to travel to the remote villages of the world to build clean water systems for undeveloped towns. We are comfortable going into communities where others have turned the street lights off. People who have Christ Consciousness know that their light is what's needed in the world. I've stated before that much of Jesus' footsteps can be traced in the 'ghettos' of Jerusalem. At one point in my ministry I was afraid of certain communities and how they would treat me as 'not one of them'. But I soon realized the greatest hurt I could have done to those communities of people was to leave them to fend for themselves; to leave them with no hope and no love. I was on the border of being labeled as "one of them Christians" in their eyes. There are numerous disinherited communities who need the utmost hope and love, yet receive the least attention.

I come in contact with innumerable persons throughout the year who are so appreciative of the fact that someone cared enough to show them love. The fact that no one forgot about them was probably the greatest display of love in their lives. As a result, it also fostered the greatest hope within them. Every month I shake the hands of homeless persons in Atlanta who say, "Pastor we appreciate what you do for us". I walk to the doors of senior citizens in our county who receive Meals on Wheels to hear the words, "young man thank you; please place the box on the counter." I have walked the streets of Atlanta at 9pm on a Friday to hear a young woman say, "I don't like selling my body, but I have to. Thank you for praying with me." On the first Sunday of each month I hear, "Pastor it is great you provide Free HIV testing for those who can't afford it". I have seen the eyes of a community light up when their new water purification system produces its first few gallons of clean drinking water. People want to know they matter. People want to know they are cared for. People want to know someone out there thinks more about others than they think about themselves. People want to know that they have not been forgotten. People want to know that their family, called humanity, still cares.

    The felon is worthy of redemption. Their one legal mistake, or multiple, judicial run ins do not disqualify them from the compassion of the Christian community. The single mother, who only has evidence of what other non-married Christians do behind closed doors, is still worthy of being embraced by the community she grew up in. The homeless person, who like many of us were just one check away from poverty, does not deserve to be ignored. The person living with HIV, whether sexually transmitted or by medical mistake, should not be viewed as the leper of biblical times. The person who is same gender loving deserves to be loved as they are, regardless if you agree with their lifestyle or not. The woman who sleeps with men for money, although some of these men are active in our churches, deserves not to be looked at as if her 'mistake' is unforgivable.

    These are just a few examples of people God is challenging us to embrace. These are a couple of the many who need our time and attention. These are those who God has commissioned us to go after and serve. If anything, these are the ones who need Christ's love showered on them the most. It is not the Pastor who needs more love. It is not the Sunday school teacher who needs more love. It is not the 11am worshipper who needs more love. It is not the person in our small groups that needs more love. It is not the choir member who needs more love. These are those who need forgiveness the most. These are those in need of kind-heartedness. However, most important of these things is that true Christians should offer these groups of people an opportunity, and environment, for redemption.

JESUS: A MAN FOR THE DISENFRANCHISED

Jesus connected with the disenfranchised. Jesus connected with those who we were taught to distance ourselves from. Let's be honest. Some of the above mentioned classes of people we have been trained to disassociate from. *Much of this perpetuated action I blame on those who carry the privilege of the platform.* I blame those who have the voice, and have the audiences, for the continued stigmas that are echoed in our community. I blame those who preach condemnation and not forgiveness. I blame those who speak about wrong but will never promote the "right thing to do". I blame those who showcase the wrongs of society and teach others to stay away from these issues.

The concern with the contemporary Christian is they do not embrace the oughts of life. The actions we ought to be taking to reconcile and connect the disenfranchised back to Christ. A person should not serve because they feel as though they have to. A true humanitarian serves because they feel as though they have an obligation, or ought, to make the world a better place. This entire text is centered on the oughts of Christianity. These are the things Christ gave us as considerations. We don't have to follow God's word to serve others, but we ought to. Listed on these pages are the things we, as True Christians, ought to be doing because we feel the pull of God on our heartstrings for the marginalized and the oppressed.

Jesus understood that to look at 'the other' was to look in the eyes of God. Jesus said, *"For I was hungry and you gave me food, I was thirsty and you gave me drink, I was a stranger and you welcomed me, I was naked and you clothed me, I was sick and you visited me, I was in prison and you came to me." (Matthew 25:35-36 ESV)* Taking care of the needs of humanity is taking care of Christ. Everything a true Christian does should feel like their responsibility to God's self. When you read the verses before this passage of scripture you will find a very perplexed and confused group of disciples. They did not understand how the Son of God could be connected to man. They did not understand how the messiah could be connected to the common man. The disciples could not fathom how this divine miracle worker could be associated with the sick and downtrodden. What Jesus teaches in his words demonstrates to us the purest form of Christ consciousness.

We, too, must train ourselves to connect with others who are not like us. There is no "other" in the eyes of God. Although we may have been influenced by others to think about some people in a negative regard, we should reflect on the fact that they possess the potential to be good. Miguel De La Torre supports this stand for the disenfranchised when he writes, "Only by loving the disenfranchised, by seeing Jesus among the poor and weak, can one learn to love Jesus who claims to be the marginalized. To love the marginalized is to love Jesus, making fellowship with God possible as one enters into just fellowship with the disenfranchised.[132]

---

[132] Torre, Miguel A De La. 2004. *Doing Christian Ethics from the Margins.* Maryknoll: Orbis Books.

JESUS AS ADVOCATE FOR THE GREATEST SENSE OF COMMUNITY

Jesus advocated for the greatest since of community. If you could collect all of Jesus' message into one phrase what could you come up with? I would say, "Humanity that lives as one, loves as one and serves as one". The prophetic writings proclaimed the messiah would be one who would usher in global peace. It was anticipated that the messiah would be a person who brought healing and restoration to the world. While Jesus did not directly accomplish this in his lifetime, his message, however, pointed us in the direction of a global community that lives in harmony with one another. Over two thousand years later we are still striving for that global community. We still have hopes for global peace.

What I believe Jesus wanted to enlighten us on was a global consciousness of the African Proverb 'I am because you are'. This age-old proverb is still displayed, and taught, in current day African derived religions and cultures. This short phrase reminds us that our presence in the world is the result of someone else's presence. As a result, our existence influences the reality of those around us; and vice versa. Wouldn't it be great to live in a world where people still look out for one another in the same way they would look out for themselves? Whether in Africa or Asia, we too should strive for this illustration of communal living. It works when we make the mindful decision to embrace this consciousness.

If we were to dissect the ministry of Jesus this thought process would slap us in the face. This principle flows through the biblical text from the environments of Abraham to Paul. Jesus was a strong activist for connecting people back to God and humanity. What we can learn from the model of Jesus is that we have been guilty of creating these pockets of separation. We have been guilty of labeling people other than ourselves as inferior. Not recognizing we all share the same divine nature. What we have not come to the realization of is that the creation of these pods is what has been killing the faith community. If I could re-coin the phrase "I am because you are" for the context of this text I would say the church is because the community is. Likewise the community is because the church is. Both cannot survive on their own. Both need one another. Both should be held responsible for the other's success. The church and the community are not just married, they are intrinsically one in the same, called to help the other maximize its highest potential.

How do we begin this process of displaying God's love as service to humanity?

Jesus, and the Prophet Isaiah, state the same authoritative words in the bible as a response to this question. *"The spirit of the Lord is upon me, because he has anointed me to proclaim good news to the poor. He has sent me to proclaim liberty to the captives and recovering of sight to the blind, to set at liberty those who are oppressed, to proclaim the year of the Lord's favor." (Luke 4:18, Isaiah 61:1)* These commanding words offer to the modern Christians an excellent point of departure for service. As I come to the close of this text I will examine the elements of this passage as a blueprint for the millennial Christian to deliberate. These words became the quintessential connection between the Old and the New Testament. As Jesus read this text in His environment, I believe we have been commissioned to echo these words for the world we live in. In the same regard, I believe these words can help us to connect the New Testament with present day culture. The rhythm of these words run parallel to the heartbeat of God. Jesus made these, past to present, connections often as He quoted the writings of many prophets, specifically Isaiah, in his teaching. Likewise we should be reading from the words of our great prophet Jesus as the authority for Christian service and humanitarian responsibility. Now we must take Jesus' message and ensure it is being carried properly until His return.

A PROCLAMATION OF GOOD NEWS TO THE POOR

The heartbeat of God must proclaim good news to the poor. We have to begin utilizing the power of our voices. A person can have resources, opportunities and environments snatched from them. But what the world can't take away from any individual is their ability to speak. Even with the threat of censorship, the proclamations of a better world cannot be tamed. What today's Christians should embrace is the art of advocacy and activism. We cannot keep the good news of Christ's love solely in our hearts. There must be a willingness to trumpet the call, and commission, of Christ. Should we choose to add to our list of desired titles in life, we should add advocate. Coupled with advocacy is also the awareness, and new sense of consciousness, needed to bring revolution to the issues of the world. There are a plethora of social justice issues which require our attention. Many of them have been outlined in this text. But how are we supposed to know what they are if there is no one out there bringing awareness to them?

With certainty, it would be foolish for one person to attempt having their hands in all the items listed in this text. While this text may motivate you to act on all things humanitarian, there is the actuality that one person cannot save humanity. While there are dozens of issues in the community that I would like to see be resolved, my church has decided to focus on five: homelessness, clean water initiatives, senior citizen connections, HIV/AIDS and human sex trafficking. I would encourage other churches to do the same. Select a few causes to focus all of your attention on and perfect those areas. I will never forget a conversation I had with one of my members where they shared that the previous ministry they attended had over 50 ministries, and auxiliaries, but only 7 were active. The same advice should be given to the modern believer, and non-believer. It would be unwise to sign up for every community service opportunity presented to you. Choose a few causes and commit your time, voice and resources to those specific things. While there should be explicit things we are involved in, we can still champion our voices to as many causes as our mouths will allow. What we can see in the life and ministry of Jesus is His voice as it called for the awareness of injustices.

What we see throughout the biblical text is Jesus bringing a new sense of realization to the issues people of his time chose to turn a blind eye to. What we can learn from Jesus' example is just because the issue doesn't affect you personally, doesn't mean the issue doesn't require our attention communally. Most of today's Christians live with the mentality of "I'm not going through it, and no one I know is going through it, so why should I care?". But what happens when you DO go through it and seek the compassion of other Christians who echo the same mindset? I don't know if we understand the cycle of selfishness we are perpetuating? I find it humorous when I speak at various conventions and conferences about the role the church has to play on educating about, and helping to end the spread of, HIV and AIDS in the community. I am often asked if I have the virus or have been effected by the epidemic. When I answer in the negative people are often puzzled as to why I made the choice to be an advocate for this community. My response is always, "why not?"

The heartbeat of God must attend to the poor. The modern Christian's efforts in the world should be philanthropic. True Christians are selfless and have the spirit of compassion towards the underprivileged. Dead Christians are selfish and are unconscious of the 'richness' God has blessed them with and their ability to share it with others. I believe when we are first exposed to the word poor we automatically think it means to not have money or material goods. What I believe the word 'poor' should point our attention to are those who ultimately need hope. Poor is relative. When the bible speaks of attending to the poor I believe it was an encouragement for us to serve the deprived; those who may not have the same resources as another.

There are so many things God has graced humanity with. One of the foremost messages I believe humanity should carry to others is that life is the greatest blessing. A large house, fancy car or six-figure income do not equate to happiness, success or being rich. The message we should take to the poor is that if God made the promise to look out for the sparrow, that same promise holds true for them. Jesus says:

> [28]"Don't be afraid of those who want to kill your body; they cannot touch your soul. Fear only God, who can destroy both soul and body in hell. [29]What is the price of two sparrows—one copper coin? But not a single sparrow can fall to the ground without your Father knowing it. [30]And the very hairs on your head are all numbered. [31]So don't be afraid; you are more valuable to God than a whole flock of sparrows. Matthew 10:28-31

We should be reminded through this text that life, each day, gives us an awareness that we still have purpose.

The poor doesn't need handouts, they need hope.

Humans are, by nature, selfish. We have been preprogrammed to take care of ourselves, and to look out for our own wellbeing, first and foremost. It takes exposure and enlightenment for a person to learn selflessness. I will never forget the first time I heard this word in my life. I was a freshman in college when a colleague of mine commended the work that I did as a minister at the time. She said, "The things you do are so selfless and should be applauded!" I originally thought she said the word selfish, but I soon discovered that this term was the best word to describe people who did what I did. While others like the terms servant, humanitarian and philanthropist, I admire those who understand that their actions are totally selfless. We have been taught since we were young to always look out for ourselves. We are even told when traveling, that in the event of an emergency to place personal safety above the safety of others. What would happen if we lived in a world that wasn't created through the 'survival of the fittest' mentality? We should learn, as True Christians, how to take care of something other than ourselves.

Care, love, compassion and concern should be at the root of our actions. If we are going to carry the torch handed to us by Christ himself it is going to require us to open our hearts to those who need it most. Henri Nouwen says, "Compassion must become the core, and even the nature, of authority. Christian leaders are people of God only insofar as they are able to make the compassion of God with humanity- which is visible in Jesus Christ- credible in their own world."[133] Christians who are centered on service are not focused on their own strength and authority. They recognize that love is what will fuel their efforts, and kindness towards humanity will be the vehicle to expand the message of Christ. Love has to be our sincere effort, and end result, when executing the great commission.

Nouwen also states, "Compassion is born when we discover in the center of our own existence, not only that God is God and humans are humans, but also that our neighbor really is our fellow human being."[134] These are not blanket statements that should be viewed as illusion. These are not lofty dreams of a better reality. These are not simply words on paper for the intent to make us feel good. This is reality. The love of God is real. The love of God has the power to transform people and systems. The love of God has the power to initiate revolutions and social causes. This love is shown in the extensions of our human service towards one another. That service is not only for the other, that service is also worship to our God.

---

[133] Nouwen, Henri J. M. 1972. *The Wounded Healer: Ministry in Contemporary Society.* New York: Doubleday Religion.

[134] Nouwen, Henri J. M. 1972. *The Wounded Healer: Ministry in Contemporary Society.* New York: Doubleday Religion.

LIBERTY AND HEALING FOR HUMANITY BEGINS IN "THE YEAR OF OUR LORD"

The heartbeat's ultimate goal should be liberty for all who are oppressed and marginalized. Our action's end result should be autonomy and freedom for those who we have connected to their condition. Many Christians in America, and around the world, have become blind to the suppression experienced throughout humanity. There are those who are pushed into the margins on a daily basis; not by choice or personal intent but by circumstance. Those that are suffering in society have become prisoners to their conditions. They have come to believe that their present circumstance has separated them from God. This assumption is far from true. What true Christians should promote is the actuality that all have the potential of being liberated from their present environment. To the same degree it should be echoed that God is aware of their conditions and wants to share in their struggle.

The felon deserves liberty from being perceived as a criminal after they have served their time. The single mother deserves liberty from being judged for having a child unmarried. The person living with HIV deserves liberty from being viewed as unclean and dirty because of their health status. The person living under the condition of homelessness deserves liberty from being assumed as a drunk, a drug addict or a mentally ill person. There are other communities not listed who deserve liberty from being labeled as something other than a child of God and extension of their creator.

Not only society, but many contemporary churches have created these prisons that do not appreciate the autonomous value of the individual. Instead, these institutions have locked their doors to communities who do not represent the status quo of society. Nonetheless, many of these societal prisons were erected through the ignorance of people. What modern Christians have done is perpetuated how they were taught to interact with these various groups. The reality is that many of us were taught to interact with oppressed communities by separating ourselves from them.

Instead of engaging with these groups of people, we were trained to disassociate ourselves from them. Instead of us offering assistance to the person living on the streets we were taught to ignore them. Instead of us offering mental support, and a way to escape to the person experiencing domestic violence, we close our curtains because we were taught that what happens in other people's houses is none of our business. As a result, not only did we place a wall between us and them, but what we ultimately created was societal prison cells that only marginalized the ones we have been created to serve.

It only takes four walls to create a room. Therefore it only takes four Christians to reject a group into isolation.

The heartbeat of God should touch the captives. The process of introducing captives back into society requires restoration and redemption. The issue I find with most modern day Christians is they forget about their process of redemption and restoration. They neglect to remember the fact that at some point they too were bound by something. Whether it was a relationship, an addiction or a mentality about our self, we have all been captivated by something. It is amazing to me how modern day Christians won't go to the degree of actually walking with the oppressed to accompany them out of their oppressed state. The attitude of "just give them Jesus and let them figure it out" is killing humanity and destroying the perception people have about Christianity. True Christians should be willing to matriculate through these processes in order to produce a whole, and restored, human being.

There must be a system which tends to the needs of the captive person. What do I mean by tending to the needs of the person? It is simple. We as True Christians should be like parents holding on to the back seat of the oppress' bicycle as they learn to ride without their training wheels for the first time. It is hard for a 3 year old learning how to ride a bike without the support of their guardian behind them. In like manner, it is a challenge for the oppressed to find their footing in society without the support of the community and the church. It is so disheartening to me at how churches will give out bibles and marketing material to promote worship, but are unwilling to make the journey with the person.

The levels of restoration and redemption should give the oppressed intrinsic and autonomous value that's within. In other words the process in which we use to liberate the captives must speak to the core of who they are. We should be affirming them, through this process of restoration, that they too are a part of the family of faith. The key to true ministry and outreach is to promote the worth of an individual beyond their present environment. The focus of True Christians should be to campaign to others for the rights and privileges of the burdened. The focus should also be to speak to the oppressed in such a way that affirms their personhood and value.

The heartbeat of God should provide healing. Nevertheless we must understand healing within itself is a process. The body has the ability to heal itself through the cooperative work of muscles, cells, blood and organs. Likewise, if the body of Christ is going to provide healing to the nations we will have to work as a community to eradicate the issues present throughout the world. As I stated in the previous section, our mission as modern Christians is to introduce the mentality of **process healing** and not **instant healing**. When a person hears the term healing, a Christian who has not been enlightened into Christ consciousness would automatically associate it with physical sickness. But when the bible speaks about healing, enlightened Christians will understand that any broken aspect of life, or our world, requires healing.

Broken relationships. Broken finances. Broken career paths. Broken families and homes. Broken educational pursuits. There are countless things in life that will leave a person broken. There are also things that will leave communities and cultures in desperate need of mending. Healing is not solely a physical experience. While it does not take long, or much, to break a person, it is a process to heal from whatever broke them. While it may be a plethora of contributors to broken systems in our communities, it will take even more contributors to right the wrongs. Christ Conscious Christians will learn to bring a positive spiritual aspect to this process.

In the same manner a cut heals on the physical body, likewise we should embrace the healing process of the oppressed and humanity. Healing often happens in stages and in layers. Taking this information into consideration, we must remain sensitive to the various healing levels we may find the oppressed. We have to recognize there are some who have recently fallen into their state of oppression and are in the beginning stages of their healing journey. We have to recognize there are people who have just commenced their journey of restoration. On the contrary we may find people who are just at the brink of redemption and need that extra push to complete their process. Regardless of the level we may discover a person, we should be thoughtful of the various stages each soul is experiencing while being sensitive to their needs.

The heartbeat of God should be aimed in the direction of the oppressed. In the same esteem as healing, eradicating oppressive behavior must be implicit as a process. It would be unwise to restore someone to the level of healed, for them to go out and revisit the same destructive behavior that broke them in the first place. Oppression doesn't happen overnight. Over time people fall into oppressed states. Often times it is the result of continuous behavior or choices made on their part. Over time people develop stereotypes and stigmas about oppressed people. Over time society tries to remedy oppression. What we should understand as

True Christians, is in order to liberate someone from oppression we must be willing to walk with others in their expedition out of oppression. We should be humans who care about the rising up of people out of oppressed states and conditions. However, we must also note that the rising action is a process within itself.

The first step, in my opinion, is relieving the pressure other Christians have placed in the system. Over time some Christians have become the issue and not the solution to these problems we face. Over time some Christians have only added to the difficult environments of marginalization. Over time some Christians have made the weight heavier on those who are trying to get a leg up. Some Christians do this with their judgements and stereotypes towards these communities. I will never forget introducing a concept to a friend of mine to end homelessness in the Atlanta area. This solution was to build tiny, and affordable, houses for this population of people. The houses would have been no larger than a few dozen square feet but they would have provided the basic necessity of a roof over one's head. Their initial response to me was, 'so how do we make sure they don't sell drugs in the houses?'. How have we become so ignorant to still make assumptions that all homeless people sell drugs, are mentally ill or substance abusers? I was expecting his response to be, 'Pastor that's a great initiative! What do we have to do to make it happen?' Instead I was met with ignorance, and an unwillingness to restore people and offer hope.

We wonder why the oppressed never rise? Some modern Christians and some contemporary churches won't allow them to. We wonder why the homeless remain homeless? Because Christians, like my friend, still assume they are all on drugs or ex-convicts. We wonder why the felon will never find employment? Because some Christians still assume what they were arrested for is unforgivable, and proves that they are a bad person unworthy of redemption; even after they have served their time. We wonder why the person living with HIV won't attend our worship experiences? Because ignorant Christians are too afraid to touch them at the altar when they come for prayer. We wonder why poverty, human sex trafficking, drug wars and social injustices remain prevalent in the world? Because a large number of modern Christians refuse to get involved in the remedy the problems.

Nonetheless we carry our bibles in the back seat of our cars and ensure we have our gold cross necklaces on before we leave the house each morning. For the traditional Christian, these two images offer comfort and familiarity. To those who may not understand the grace of God in their life daily, these symbols represent another type, and level, of hope. To the oppressed and the marginalized these are not mere religious images. Miguel De La Torre says:

> "The importance of the cross for the marginalized is that they have a God who understands their trials and tribulations because God in the flesh also suffered trials and tribulations. The good news is not so much that Jesus was crucified, but that Jesus rose from the dead, not to demonstrate God's power, but to provide hope to today's crucified that they too will be ultimately victorious over the oppression they face."[135]

I could not have said it any better than this. For those who preach the message of the cross on Sunday mornings we cannot neglect the fact that Jesus did the one thing every human will do; He died. There is no greater realization of mortality that to taste death. With this in mind, the death of Christ was a reminder that the Divine was willing to intentionally sip from the cup of the mortal. The glory, in the resurrection of Christ, was to remind us that this consciousness we call life has the potential to be dramatically altered when we tap into the ultimate energy of God. Jesus was resurrected to remind us that dead situations can live when we give our lives as an extension of God's work and presence here on earth.

---

[135] Torre, Miguel A De La. 2004. *Doing Christian Ethics from the Margins*. Maryknoll: Orbis Books.

If modern millennial Christians want to help the oppressed and the marginalized, our primary responsibility is to relieve their pressure with the love of Christ.

The heartbeat of God must operate continuously as 'the year of the Lord'. There is no time for breaks. The work of God is crucial and continuous. The work of Christ cannot happen with delay. To me this is the most important element of the scripture as it relates to Christ's message of Social Justice. We can talk about doing the work of God, or we can do the work of God. However, this work has to begin now. The work outlined in this text, and the Christ consciousness associated with it, starts the moment we say "yes". God's timing is now timing. Many Christians have been waiting for someone else to do the work. True Christians should be on fire to initiate the movement now!

One practice I have adopted as a millennial Christian is to act when I see injustices being perpetrated. The moment I hear about a problem or injustice that involves the oppressed or the marginalized my conscious begins to contemplate what needs to be done. I understand I can't act on everything. On the other hand, what I can do, I am unafraid to get involved with. What I have come to embrace is my role, and my part, in the solution of the problems my communities face; and communities around the globe. I ask myself often, "Will I be a part of the remedy, or will my silence only propagate the problem?" An irrelevant Christian can blame ignorance, or lack of resources, to their noninvolvement with social issues. A True Christian, once they become aware of the cries of humanity, should have a new sense of accountability and responsibility to act expeditiously.

Jesus' message for a change was a message of "accomplishment here and now". Jesus addressed issues and spoke truth to power in the moment injustices presented themselves. He spoke when others would have wanted him to be silent.

Nevertheless, he spoke on behalf of the people whose voices would have never made it to the ears of those who had the influence to make change. Jesus never held His tongue or said "let me wait this one out". Rather Jesus jumped on the chopping block of the marginalized and transformed that block into his pulpit for change and transformation in the community. Jesus did not just speak to the oppressed, He spoke for the oppressed.

For Augustine, grace did not free the moral agent from his or her obligation to perform good works; in fact, conversion generated a new creature in Christ now capable of doing good because his or her life was dominated by God's grace.[136] What we discover, in various stories where Jesus took up for the oppressed, is this commission for the delivered to leave their condition and share their new found grace with someone else. We can recall the woman who was caught in adultery in John 8:1-11:

> [1]Jesus returned to the Mount of Olives, [2]but early the next morning he was back again at the Temple. A crowd soon gathered, and he sat down and taught them. [3]As he was speaking, the teachers of religious law and the Pharisees brought a woman who had been caught in the act of adultery. They put her in front of the crowd. [4]"Teacher," they said to Jesus, "this woman was caught in the act of adultery. [5]The law of Moses says to stone her. What do you say?" [6]They were trying to trap him into saying something they could use against him, but Jesus stooped down and wrote in the dust with his finger. [7]They kept demanding an answer, so he stood up again and said, "All right, but let the one who has never sinned throw the first stone!" [8]Then he stooped down again and wrote in the dust. [9]When the accusers heard this, they slipped away one by one, beginning with the oldest, until only Jesus was left in the middle of the crowd with the woman. [10]Then Jesus stood up again and said to the woman, "Where are your accusers? Didn't even one of them condemn you?" [11]"No, Lord," she said. And Jesus said, "Neither do I. Go and sin no more."

---

[136] Kripalani, Krishna. 2004. *Mahatma Gandhi: All Men Are Brothers Autobiographical Reflections*. New York: The Continuum International Publishing Group.

Either we can be a people who wait, and talk, and meet, and plan, or we can be a people of action and change.

METHODS AND PRACTICES OF OUTREACH AND RELEVANCY

Our time together is coming to a close. I pray, if nothing else, this text has made you more aware of the present issues that are happening around the globe. I pray the information in this text has, in some way, touched your heart to become active humanitarians in the work that still must be done around the world. It is my prayer that you have a greater sense of responsibility; but more importantly that you would hold yourself more accountable as a champion for Christ's message about service.

I wrote this text with the intent of reaching the millennial Christian and those who seek a closer relationship with the community. But as I discussed in the previous chapter, the time for the manifestation of these ideas is now. Whether you are reading this text in 2015 or 2050 our responsibility remains the same: To serve the current needs of humanity. But how?

Miguel De La Torre recommends that, "The Hermeneutical Circle for Ethics includes: 1. Observing (Historical and Interpretive Analysis, 2. Reflecting (Social Analysis), 3. Praying (Theological and Biblical Analysis, 4. Acting (Implementation of Praxis, and 5. Reassessing (New Ethical Perspectives)"[137] I would agree with this

---

[137] Torre, Miguel A De La. 2004. *Doing Christian Ethics from the Margins.* Maryknoll: Orbis Books.

method and approach to service. We must first take the back seat as witnesses to the social and humanitarian issues that face our globe. We should be willing to observe our past struggles in a way to prepare for future successes. We should be laser focused on what can been seen outside the four walls of the church. After observation there ought to be a moment of reflection and consideration. This reflection is not limited to thinking about these issues presented before us, but should also include personal reflection as to our role in the solution. This would involve a conversation with our selves as well as our Creator. This is why prayer before action is so important. We are able to communicate with the assignment giver in such a way where we have clear instruction as to our responsibilities and strategy. Once we receive our marching orders we are able to act effectively, and in the right direction. It would be unwise for any of us to act on behalf of God without listening to the voice of God or using the bible as our primary resource. Once we have completed our assignment, we re-enter the reflective pool as we assess our actions, thoughts, successes and failures with the hope of producing new methods and strategies in the future.

There are a few biblical consideration I believe we should make as we move forward. Paul, a major biblical New Testament writer reminds us that, "If one member (of the community) suffers, with it suffer all members, or if one member is glorified, with it all members rejoice" (1 Cor. 12:26) Community occurs when the faith community gathers to stand in solidarity, sharing the trials and joys of the human condition.[138] We are in this travail together. Our primary methods of execution involves communities coming together, as one, with the shared focus and intent to accomplish something together. With that common goal, we unify through the obstacles and triumphs we endure along the road.

---

[138] Torre, Miguel A De La. 2004. *Doing Christian Ethics from the Margins.* Maryknoll: Orbis Books.

To create a more perfect world it is going to take collective effort. The same model we saw in the early church should carry over to our practices today. We should be encouraging people to come together and to bring their resources, talents, skills and networks to the table in order to advocate for change. What we can learn from the early church is that we will accomplish more as a team of Christ Conscious people than we would as personally conscious individuals. Dr. Lawrence Carter supports this proponent when he states that, "Every person ought to assist in the realization of maximum value in other persons, respecting all persons as ends in themselves, with due respect for their dignity as autonomous centers of value appraisal and experience, and, as far as possible, cooperate with others in the production and enjoyment of shared values.[139]

However, it will not just require us to cooperate. It will require us to adopt the spirit of sympathy and empathy for those who are oppressed and marginalized. This is the foundation for genuine compassion. We have to place ourselves in the shoes of those we have been called to serve. We should think of methods and strategies that fit the environments we have been challenged to help. Our actions should consider those we have been commissioned to serve. We should not press for things that are comfortable for us to accomplish. Rather we should seek solutions that answer the needs of those communities that need our support. Carter says that "Imagining and feeling yourself in someone else's shoes is the basis for shared human experience."[140] We cannot claim to be in the fight with the oppressed and the marginalized if we are unable to walk a day in their reality. We cannot be effective if we are unwilling to dialogue with them in order to uncover the root of their hurt and

---

[139] Carter, Lawrence Edward, George David Miller, and Neelakanta Radhakrishnan. 2001. *Global Ethical Options*. Trumbull: Weatherhill.

[140] Carter, Lawrence Edward, George David Miller, and Neelakanta Radhakrishnan. 2001. *Global Ethical Options*. Trumbull: Weatherhill.

condition. We share this reality called earth. Likewise we should be willing to share the burdens of the world.

The bible gives us the golden rule to love others and to love God in all we do. This remains the standard of our service consciousness. This, coupled with the more well know "golden rule", to do unto others as you would have them do unto you, offer us a great point of departure for our methods and service practices. Dr. Carter also lets us know that, "The Golden Rule encourages us to see more than ourselves when making ethical decisions. The world is not a big mirror, reflecting back our image and needs. Facing the world is facing others. Facing others is facing ourselves, because there is no other, no separation."[141] In other words when we love on others we are loving on God. When we commit to serving others we are committing to serving the well-being of all humanity. When we advocate for one group in a specific environment we are raises our voices for all who experience that reality in communities around the globe. Rooting for change in policies, systems and ideologies that keep people oppressed and marginalized in one state is to push for social and systematic change across the waters of the world.

We return to the execution of altruism, or selflessness. Altruism is our connectedness with others. These Golden Rules encourage us to reflect on the needs of others in our quest to create a more perfect world. These rules compel us to extend our viewpoint from personal well-being to the well-being of others. Altruistic acts may range from small gestures such as: politeness, providing a fast food meal to a homeless family, donating your gently used clothing to a transitional program for women leaving domestic abuse environments, or volunteering for your local meals on wheels program. Altruistic gestures have the potential to grow to grand gestures

---

[141] Carter, Lawrence Edward, George David Miller, and Neelakanta Radhakrishnan. 2001. *Global Ethical Options*. Trumbull: Weatherhill.

such as living with only enough to survive and sending the rest of one's income to starving peoples. In either regard, more selfless acts are needed in the world.

> In a conversation with Rev. Dr. Lawrence E. Carter he says, Ethical codes direct us to pay attention to the needs of others. We must learn to act on the behalf of others instead of the present and future self (individual). Personal identification with personal morality is viably important. The rights and obligations of all persons work, or act together effectively. Human rights are not demands. Our relationship is one of service, not one of making demands. We all have the right to participate in this moral stand for human welfare. It matters what the "act" brings into being. We must know that our actions will produce a virtue within itself and on its own. Altruism does not tell us what value in others to promote. There is not an automatic cultural content. Altruism is a democratic engagement that bridges the works of others and their diverse interest. A responsible participation in common interest. It is about love and justice, respect of persons, and a motivation of goodwill towards the holistic needs of other persons as ones own.[142]

> In another conversation I had with my Pastor Dr. William E. Flippin, he echoes the spiritual truth that it will take transformational leadership in order to re-establish the relevancy of the church and Christianity. This transformation is a biblical principle and is rooted in that spiritual formation (2 Corinthians 3:18 and 5:17, Ephesians 5:8). This transformation is produced through the empowering work of the Holy Spirit (2 Thessalonians 2:13 and John 14:26). We must believe this transformation is possible. It is the belief that the best is yet to come (Luke 1:37 and Matthew 21:22). The transformation begins in the heart of the people (Romans 12:2). This transformation must be intentional. Nothing is created in chaos (Luke 10:1-3 and Acts 13:46). Finally, we must understand that this transformation is a process (Philippians 1:6, 2 Corinthians 3:14 and Hebrews 6:11)[143]

---

[142] Rev. Dr. Lawrence E. Carter, Sr., interview by Dr. Wendel T. Dandridge. 2016. *Dean of The Martin Luther King Jr. International Ecumenical Chapel on the Campus of Morehouse College* (April 19).

[143] Flippin, Dr. William E., interview by Dr. Wendel T. Dandridge. 2016. *Pastor of The Greater Piney Grove Baptist Church* (April 19).

Gene Wilkes recommends a 5 step process, coupled with scripture, to equip others:

1. **Encourage them to serve**

"For you were called to freedom, brothers. Only do not use your freedom as an opportunity for the flesh, but through love serve one another." (Galatians 5:13)

2. **Qualify them to serve**

[6]He has enabled us to be ministers of his new covenant. This is a covenant not of written laws, but of the Spirit. The old written covenant ends in death; but under the new covenant, the Spirit gives life. (2 Cor. 3:6)

3. **Understand their needs**

[1]Once Jesus was in a certain place praying. As he finished, one of his disciples came to him and said, "Lord, teach us to pray, just as John taught his disciples." [2]Jesus said, "This is how you should pray: "Father, may your name be kept holy. May your Kingdom come soon. [3]Give us each day the food we need, [4]and forgive us our sins, as we forgive those who sin against us. And don't let us yield to temptation."(Luke 11:1-4)

4. **Instruct them**

[18]Jesus came and told his disciples, "I have been given all authority in heaven and on earth. [19]Therefore, go and make disciples of all the nations, baptizing them in the name of the Father and the Son and the Holy Spirit. [20]Teach these new disciples to obey all the commands I have given you. And be sure of this: I am with you always, even to the end of the age." (Matthew 28: 18-20)

5. **Pray for them**

[6]"I have revealed you to the ones you gave me from this world. They were always yours. You gave them to me, and they have kept your word. [7]Now they know that everything I have is a gift from you, [8]for I have passed on to them the message you gave me. They accepted it and know that I came from you, and they believe you sent me. [9]"My prayer is not for the world, but for those you have given me, because they belong to you. [10]All who are mine belong to you, and you have given them to me, so they bring me glory. [11]Now I am departing from the world; they are staying in this world, but I am coming to you. Holy Father, you have given me your name; now protect them by the power of your name so that they will be united just as we are. [12]During my time here, I protected them by the power

of the name you gave me. I guarded them so that not one was lost, except the one headed for destruction, as the Scriptures foretold. [13]"Now I am coming to you. I told them many things while I was with them in this world so they would be filled with my joy. [14]I have given them your word. And the world hates them because they do not belong to the world, just as I do not belong to the world. [15]I'm not asking you to take them out of the world, but to keep them safe from the evil one. [16]They do not belong to this world any more than I do. [17]Make them holy by your truth; teach them your word, which is truth. [18]Just as you sent me into the world, I am sending them into the world. [19]And I give myself as a holy sacrifice for them so they can be made holy by your truth (John 17:6-19)

In it he prayed for their unity (v. 11). He prayed that they would have joy in ministry (v. 13). Jesus prayed for their protection (v. 15). He prayed that they remain holy, set apart, by the truth of God's Word (v. 17). Jesus equipped his disciples by praying for them.[144]

According to another advocate in this text, Henri J. M. Nouwen, there are basic principles of Christian leadership: first, personal concern, which asks people to give their lives for others; second, a deep-rooted faith in the value and meaning of life, even when the days look dark; and third, an out-going hope that always looks for tomorrow, even beyond the moment of death. And all these principles are based on the one and only conviction that, since God has become human, it is human beings who have the power to lead their fellows to freedom.[145] Each of these principles has a place in our contemporary thought and actions. The concern we should have for others is quintessential to carry out the work we have for Christ. We must learn to value people in such a way where they mean something to the world and the

---

[144] Wilkes, C. Gene. 1998. *Jesus on Leadership: Discovering the Secrets of Servant Leadership from the Life of Christ.* Wheaton: Tyndale House Publishers.

[145] Nouwen, Henri J. M. 1972. *The Wounded Healer: Ministry in Contemporary Society.* New York: Doubleday Religion.

environments they are in. At the end of the day we should have a goal to establish hope in our communities.

My push is not for you to go to church more. My push is not for you to read the bible more. My push is not for you to pray more. My push is not for you to meditate more. While these acts of faith, and practices, are a part of our religious journey, my push is for you to devote yourself to be the heartbeat of God here on earth. To be the hands, feet and representation of God's love, grace and mercy to humanity. My push is for you to be conscious of the community, and humanitarian, work you are a part of. My push is for you to make serving others a lifestyle. My push is for you to live these principles and recommendations in such a way that it inspires others to serve as well. My push is to create active Christians who have a heart for service. My push it to re-establish church and Christian relevancy through community service, social justice and humanitarian service.

Let's be honest, if you are reading this text you are more than likely in the generational classification of the millennials. I have referred to this group often in this text. However, where you classification is millennial, baby boomer, generation XYZ, or born in the year 2050, the message of Christ remains the same. Many of us may have been raised in church, or are constantly being told to go to church. But you don't attend church. It's not because you don't like church, or appreciate the spiritual necessity of worship, you just don't see the church doing what you believe they should be doing in the community and the globe. You would love to be connected to a church that feeds you spiritually. But then again you also desire a ministry that will allow you to work and serve humanity. Christian Chiakulas, in this text "Churches could fill their pews with millennials if they just did this" writes that, *"Many people my age are simply not interested in church, organized religion or religion in general, and no number of projectors, hip, youthful pastors, or twitter hashtags are going to change that."*[146] Let's face the facts, **you as a person who values service and spirituality does not want to become an irrelevant Christian yourself.** You may be saying to yourself, "I miss church, but I have yet to find a ministry doing what I believe the church should be doing. I want to be involved. I also have not found a church that helps be to embrace my personal humanity and journey to enlightenment."

However, Christian also writes, "I know from experience that there are huge numbers of millennials that are open to organized religion, and in fact are yearning from a church that they feel comfortable devoting their time and spiritual energy towards."[147] The church, and the Christian faith, should see the golden pot at the end of the rainbow called service. We have not lost today's generation and we will not run the risk of losing future generations if we strive towards this Christ consciousness. I encounter people every day who are tired of churches that do nothing for the community. However they are still searching for a place to belong spirituallty. Instead of raising their concern to Pastors and church leadership, present day millennials have chosen to disassociate themselves from organized religion all together. However, after I launched The Worship Center in Atlanta I came across countless people who were desperately looking for opportunities to serve and give back. This is only to be seen as an illustration, but the zombies of Christianity are ready to receive life! There are countless persons who want to connect back to God through service. But more importantly, society in general is prepared to connect back to humanity!

---

[146] Chiakulas, Christian. 2015. *Churches could fill their pews with millennials if they just did this.* September 30. www.huffingtonpost.com/christian-chiakulas/churches-millennials-if-they-just-did-this_b_8215846.html.

[147] Chiakulas, Christian. 2015. *Churches could fill their pews with millennials if they just did this.* September 30. www.huffingtonpost.com/christian-chiakulas/churches-millennials-if-they-just-did-this_b_8215846.html.

Modern Christians are looking for a way to connect to the message of Jesus. They are searching for the church to manifest itself in the heart of the community. I believe that modern, and millennial, Christians are looking for a way to not just 'be' Christians, but for a way to do the work of Christ. We can note that these Christians have studied the bible for themselves and are appalled at how traditional Christians have contributed very little to the world. True Christians have read the words of Jesus and are bold enough to do the courageous things Jesus did.

True Christians are Christians who were tired of living but not giving life.

I was, like many of you, tired of the romanticized Jesus. I was tired of the Jesus who smiled and kissed the children every day. I was tired of seeing traditional Christians at Thanksgiving and Christmas but never noticed them serving throughout the remainder of the year. I was tired of preachers preaching messages about grace, love, and forgiveness, but never teaching application and action around the globe. I was seeing church after church, ministry after ministry, and traditional Christian after traditional Christian doing nothing to eradicate the social injustices held in their own communities, let alone with world. As Christian further states in his text, "Millennials are not interested in a celestial Jesus with a permanent smile and open arms, unconcerned with the goings-on of planet earth. We've heard about that Jesus our entire lives, and we're not buying it."[148] These words may come across as very blunt. However, I have come in contact with many modern spiritual persons who share the same sentiment. They are tired of Jesus being painted in the lens of being primarily humble and meek. They desire a Christ who is able to relate to their personal needs as well as the needs of others. They are not buying the Jesus who didn't speak out

---

[148] Chiakulas, Christian. 2015. *Churches could fill their pews with millennials if they just did this.* September 30. www.huffingtonpost.com/christian-chiakulas/churches-millennials-if-they-just-did-this_b_8215846.html.

about the injustices of his time. Rather they seek to see manifested in today's world the type of Jesus who stands up for the oppressed and marginalized.

As a Lead Pastor and religious leader I stopped buying it, and in return started putting something else on the menu to offer the modern Christian.

Christian continues by saying, "Do you know what we would buy? Jesus the man, Jesus the prophet, the Jesus that fashioned a whip of cords and overturned the tables of the money changers for making God's house a den of robbers. The Jesus that challenged the establishment and paid the ultimate price. The Jesus that took up the cross of the poor, the weak and the marginalized in the name of God"[149] There are people in search for the revolutionary Jesus. There are people who are searching for the Jesus who was not passive in the community. There are people who are in search for the Jesus who spoke truth to power and was unapologetic about it. This is the type of Jesus the contemporary Christians desires to follow. This radical approach to human agency is consistent with the mentality of the present day millennial.

As we look out into the world and observe the injustices that are happening around us, let us make note of the countless millennials that are in the streets, holding up signs, starting protest and literally stopping highway traffic to prove their point. Is not this the type of radicalism Jesus would have applauded today in order to eradicate the problems and concerns of humanity? The radical, the bold, the courageous, the dirty and marginalized desire the radical message of Jesus! You cannot pull the wool over the eyes of the contemporary Christians the same way people have pulled the white sheet over the eyes of traditional Christians. Jesus Christ was a man of revolutionary action.

---

[149] Chiakulas, Christian. 2015. *Churches could fill their pews with millennials if they just did this.* September 30. www.huffingtonpost.com/christian-chiakulas/churches-millennials-if-they-just-did-this_b_8215846.html.

The problem with Christianity, and the church today, has nothing to do with the style of worship or the message of the church. Where the greatest rub takes place is how the message of Jesus manifests itself in the world. Traditional Christians will attend church all day. Traditional Christians will go to church and denomination conferences all year. Traditional Christians will stay at home and pray while those on the streets are the ones who need their prayers most. Traditional Christians will read books on how to fundraise and build better sanctuaries while God is challenging us to build alters in the world. Traditional Christians will go to bible study but will never sign up for an international mission's trip. Nevertheless I believe there is a generation of Christians who will become God's human agents and act while experiencing this consciousness called life.

Christian also wrote in his blog, "I'm all for love and a personal relationship with God, but I choose to follow the man who teaches that political action is worship, that social justice is love."[150] I've stated it consistently throughout this book. If certain issues, and the awareness of social injustices, do not move you into action you should turn in your Christian Card. There is much more to Christianity than communal worship and personal devotion. The primary reason the first Christians received the credibility they received was because of their social involvement.

There was one key event in history that Christians believed separated Jesus from all of the other prophets. It wasn't his words. It wasn't his actions. It wasn't his miracles. It wasn't even his death. The main event that separates Jesus from all the other prophets before him is the belief in his resurrection. What will separate True Christians from Dead Christians? It won't be their words. It won't be their

---

[150] Chiakulas, Christian. 2015. *Churches could fill their pews with millennials if they just did this.* September 30. www.huffingtonpost.com/christian-chiakulas/churches-millennials-if-they-just-did-this_b_8215846.html.

involvement in worship experiences. It won't be the healings and deliverances. It will be their involvement, and resurrection, in the thread of humanity.

People are listening for the heartbeat of God.

People are looking for ways to connect back to God and humanity. The Question is much larger than "Dead Christians: Where is the Heartbeat of God". I believe if Dead Christians continue acting (or should I say non-acting) in the way they have been, the question will ultimately become "Where is God?"

References

Aristotle. 1997. *Nichomachean Ethics*. London: Wordsworth.

Baily, Sarah Pulliam. 2015. *Christianity faces sharp decline as Americans are becoming even less affiliated with religion*. May 12. www.washingtonpost.com/news/acts-of-faith/wp/2015/05/12/christianity-faces-sharp-decline-as-americans-are-becoming-even-less-affiliated-with-religion/.

Berscheid, Ellen. n.d. "Interpersonal Modes of Knowing." In *Learning and Teaching the Ways of Knowing*, by Eisner, 60-76.

Boff, George V. Pixley & Clodovis. 1989. *The Bible, the Church, and the Poor*. Maryknoll: Orbis Books.

Boys, Mary C. 1989. *Educating in Faith*. Lima: Academic Renewal Press.

Buber, Martin. 1970. *I and Thou*. New York: Klaus Reprint.

Burns, James MacGregor. 1978. *Leadership*. New York: Harper & Row.

Carter, Lawrence Edward, George David Miller, and Neelakanta Radhakrishnan. 2001. *Global Ethical Options*. Trumbull: Weatherhill.

Center for Disease Control and Prevention. 2015. *Basic Statistics*. September 14. www.cdc.gov/hiv/statistics/basics.html.

Centers for Disease Control and Prevention. 2015. *Global WASH Fast Facts*. June 5. www.cdc.gov/healthywater/global/wash_statistics.html.

Chiakulas, Christian. 2015. *Churches could fill their pews with millennials if they just did this*. September 30. www.huffingtonpost.com/christian-chiakulas/churches-millennials-if-they-just-did-this_b_8215846.html.

DePree, Max. 1997. *Leading without Power*. San Francisco: Jossey-Bass.

Do Something Organization. n.d. *11 Facts about Human Trafficking*. www.dosomething.org/facts/11-facts-about-human-trafficking.

Dussel, Enrique. 1988. *Ethics and Community Trans. Robert R. Barr*. Maryknoll: Orbis Books.

Elliott, Harrison S. 1940. *Can Religious Education Be Christian?* New York: Macmillan.

Flippin, Dr. William E., interview by Wendel T. Dandridge. 2016. *Pastor of The Greater Piney Grove Baptist Church* (April 19).

Ford, Leif Coorlim and Dana. 2015. *Sex Trafficking: The New American slavery*. July 21. www.cnn.com/2015/07/20/us/sex-trafficking/.

Gremillion, Joseph. 1976. *The Gospel of Peace and Justice: Catholic Social Teaching Since Pope John*. Maryknoll: Orbis.

Gutierrez, Gustavo. 1998. *Liberation Theology and the Future of the Poor*. Minneapolis: Fortress Press.

Haight, Roger D. 1979. "The 'Established' Church as Mission: The Relation of the Church to the Modern World." *The Jurist 39* (The Jurist #() 11-19.

Huffington Post. 2015. *The U. S. Illiteracy Rate Hasnt Changed in 10 Years*. October 2. www.huffingtonpost.com/2013/09/06/illiteracy-rate_n_3880355.html.

Kilough, Clyde. 2015. *Why is Christianity Becoming Irrelevant?* http://lifehopeandtruth.com/change/the-church/why-is-christianity-becoming-irrelevant/.

Kouzes, James M., and Barry Z. Posner. 1994. *The Leadership Challenge*. New York: Warner Books.

Kripalani, Krishna. 2004. *Mahatma Gandhi: All Men Are Brothers Autobiographical Reflections*. New York: The Continuum International Publishing Group.

Lacan, Jacques. 1977. *Ecrits: A Selection. Trans. Alan Sheridan*. New York: W. W. Norton.

McNeill, Donald P, Douglas A Morrison, and Henri J. M. Nouwen. 1983. *Compassion: A Reflection on the Christian Life*. New York: Doubleday.

Murren, Doug. 1994. *Leadershift*. Ventura: Regal.

National Alliance to End Homelessness. 2015. *The State of Homelessness in America 2015*. April 1. www.endhomelessness.org/library/entry/the-state-of-homelessness-in-america-2015.

National Coalition Against Domestic Violence. n.d. *Statistics*. www.ncadv.org/learn/statistics.

Nazworth, Napp. 2015. *CP U.S.* May 15. www.christianpost.com/news/is-christian-decline-in-america-due-to-fewer-incognito-atheists-like-russsell-moore-said-cp-asked-pew-research-for-the-answer-139133/.

Nouwen, Henri J. M. 1972. *The Wounded Healer: Ministry in Contemporary Society*. New York: Doubleday Religion.

Quigley, Bill. 2015. *10 Facts About Homelessness.* January 18. www.economyincrisis.org/content/10-facts-about-homelessness.

Rev. Dr. Lawrence E. Carter, Sr., interview by Wendel T. Dandridge. 2016. *Dean of The Martin Luther King Jr. International Ecumenical Chapel on the Campus of Morehouse College* (April 19).

Royce, Josiah. 1995. *The Philosophy of Loyalty.* Nashville: Vanderbilt University Press.

Stetzer, Ed. 2014. *3 Reasons People are not Involved in Your Church.* June. http://www.christianitytoday.com/edstetzer/2014/june/3-reasons-people-are-not-involved-in-your-church.html.

Torre, Miguel A De La. 2004. *Doing Christian Ethics from the Margins.* Maryknoll: Orbis Books.

Unknown. 2015. *Here are 3 reasons no one is joining your church (plus one more).* October 13. www.reluctantxian.wordpress.com/2015/10/13/here-are-3-reasons-no-one-is-joining-your-church-plus-one-more.

Vagianos, Alanna. 2015. *30 Shocking Domestic Violence Statistics that Remins us its an epidemic.* February 13. www.huffingtonpost.com/2014/10/23/domestic-violence-statistics_n_5959776.html.

Water.org. n.d. *Millions Lack Safe Water.* www.water.org/water-crisis/water-facts/water/.

Wilkes, C. Gene. 1998. *Jesus on Leadership: Discovering the Secrets of Servant Leadership from the Life of Christ.* Wheaton: Tyndale House Publishers.

X, Malcolm. 1968. "The Leverett House Forum of March 18, 1964." In *The Speeches of Malcolm X at Harvard.* New York: William Morrow & Company.

Made in the USA
Monee, IL
13 February 2021